W0081991

MAJOR TRENDS IN FORMATIVE JUDAISM

1.23.84

for Lou,

Warm regards,

Jack

Program in Judaic Studies
Brown University
BROWN JUDAIC STUDIES
Edited by

Jacob Neusner,
Wendell S. Dietrich, Ernest S. Frerichs,
Alan Zuckerman

Editorial Board

David Blumenthal, Emory University (Approaches to Medieval Judaism)
Lenn Evan Goodman, University of Hawaii (Studies in Medieval Judaism)
William Scott Green, University of Rochester (Approaches to Ancient Judaism)
Martin Hengel, University of Tübingen (Hellenistic Judaism)
David Hirsch, Brown University (Modern Jewish Literature)
Baruch A. Levine, New York University (Ancient Israel)
Alan Mintz, University of Maryland (Hebrew Literature)
Valentin Nikiprowetzky, University of Paris (Ancient Judaism)
Marc L. Raphael, Ohio State University (Approaches to Judaism in Modern Times)
Peter Schäfer, University of Cologne (Ancient Judaism)
Jonathan Z. Smith, University of Chicago (Studia Philonica)
Uriel Tal, Tel Aviv University (Modern Judaism)
David Vital, Tel Aviv University (Modern Judaism)
Geza Vermes, University of Oxford (Ancient Judaism)

Corresponding Editors

David Altshuler, George Washington University
Alan J. Avery-Peck, Tulane University
Baruch M. Bokser, Dropsie University
Joel Gereboff, Arizona State University
David Goldenberg, Dropsie University
Robert Goldenberg, State University of New York, Stony Brook
David Goodblatt, Haifa University
Peter Haas, Vanderbilt University
Martin Jaffee, University of Virginia
Shamai Kanter, Temple Beth El, Rochester, New York
Jack L. Lightstone, Concordia University
Irving Mandelbaum, University of Texas, Austin
Ivan Marcus, Jewish Theological Seminary of America
Louis E. Newman, Carleton College
Gary G. Porton, University of Illinois
Richard S. Sarason, Hebrew Union College–Jewish Institute of Religion, Cincinnati
Lawrence Schiffman, New York University
Tzvee Zahavy, University of Minnesota

Editorial Committee

Roger Brooks
Paul Flesher
Howard Schwartz
Judith Romney Wegner

Number 60

MAJOR TRENDS IN FORMATIVE JUDAISM
Society and Symbol in Political Crisis

by
Jacob Neusner

MAJOR TRENDS IN FORMATIVE JUDAISM
Society and Symbol in Political Crisis

by
Jacob Neusner

Scholars Press
Chico, California

MAJOR TRENDS IN FORMATIVE JUDAISM
Society and Symbol in Political Crisis

by
Jacob Neusner

© 1983
Brown University

Library of Congress Cataloging in Publication Data

Neusner, Jacob, 1932–
    Major trends in formative Judaism.

    (Brown Judaic studies ; no. 60)
    Includes index.
    1. Judaism—History—Talmudic period, 10–425.
2. Messiah—History of doctrines. 3. Mishneh—Criticism,
interpretation, etc. I. Title. II. Series.
BM177.N477 1983   296.3'09'015   83–20176
ISBN 0–89130–668–4

Printed in the United States of America

For

Aaron and Elinor Ross Diamond

Dear friends and fellow-travellers

CONTENTS

PREFACE

The formative age of Judaism begins with the creation of the Mishnah in the first two centuries of the Common Era, and concludes with the closure of the Talmud of Babylonia in the sixth and seventh centuries. During that period of half a millenium the fundamental symbolic structure of what we now know as Judaism took shape. Since, as I shall briefly note in Chapter One, the period finds definition in events that fundamentally redefined the social and political condition of Israel, the Jewish nation, as well as of the Land of Israel, the Jews' country, we deal with a political crisis. What we want to know about the cultural-religious system framed by rabbis during the period at hand is how, if at all, the symbolic structure of Judaism relates to the political crisis of the Jewish nation.

The symbols at hand convey a profoundly religious message, but all of them serve political purposes as well. The first ones to be discussed are the symbols that served to encapsulate the governing empires of historical time: Babylonia, Media, Greece, and Rome. These by definition constitute political entities, and the statement made through identification of these empires with various symbols formed a political judgment. At the same time, given the heightened imagination of Israelite apocalypse, each symbol spoke also about God's judgment of the great empires. Accordingly, when we speak of political change, by definition we take up symbols of that change -- whatever other meaning attaches to the symbols at hand. The further symbols under discussion capture aspects of Israel's inner life but, no less than the first set, also address political realities. I refer to three symbols: Messiah, history, and Torah. The first two, of course, really form a single symbolic system, which purports to select what is eventful and consequential among the infinite number of possibilities -- things that happen -- and to show the meaningful connections, the rules that govern. That defines history as a mode of social symbolization. The conception of history comes prior to the ideology, or theology, presented by the substance of that conception. In the case of Israel's diverse cultural-religious systems, we often find joined the theory that events add up to history and bear quite specific meaning to the theory that history will come to an end with the appearance of an anointed king or priest or wonder-worker, commonly called a messiah, or the Messiah. In the case of the system created by the third- and fourth-century rabbis of the Land of Israel and of Babylonia, the definition of the Messiah conforms to the larger theses -- the points of insistence -- of the system as a whole. Hence, as I said, history and messiah constitute a single symbol, in two integrated aspects.

The other symbol, this one distinctive to and definitive of the Rabbinic mode of Judaism, is "Torah." That symbol bears a range of interrelated meanings. The only one under discussion here is Torah as a symbol of Israel's salvation. The relationship of the symbols of messiah to Torah then is clear. Each deals with the same issue, and the two have to come together to constitute and spell out the teleology of the system of which they define principal parts.

- 1 -

This statement of the basic problem of this book -- the relationship of political crisis to social symbols -- also serves to explain how these essays come together to form a single continuous statement. I begin with an account of what I conceive to be the political crisis confronting the nation of Israel in the Land of Israel in the fourth century. I mean also to provide a small example of how the symbols that emerge in the age of that crisis demand analysis and interpretation, a route into the study of a profound and complex problem.

I then proceed to the inquiry into symbols of a society speaking about itself. I begin with an unsuccessful symbol, by which I mean a symbol that in no way stood for, or evoked, sentiments or conceptions beyond itself. At issue is "the city," an abstract and powerful symbol in our own civilization, one that evokes a whole way of life and thought, but one which, for the Rabbinic documents under study, stood for little more than a mode of social description. Bearing little consequence beyond its own facts, "the city" did not constitute a significant symbol in the documents at hand.

I then turn to the three symbols that did succeed -- messiah, history, and Torah -- and, as I said, trace the standing of each of them in parts of the thick strata of the formative age of Judaism.

I conclude, as is my way, with some observations on contemporary matters, in this case the fate of the definitive symbol of Judaism: Torah. I ask what has happened to Torah among people who "study Torah" as an avocation, as a primary expression of their relationship to God. In so doing, I mean to point toward a set of questions about society and symbol in the contemporary political crisis of the Jewish nation. But, of course, working in the earlier formative age, I do not have to deal with the critical issues of the newest period in the ongoing formation of Judaism.

In inaugurating these studies of problems and topics in formative Judaism, I announce my conviction that we now have reached the stage at which we may describe, analyze, and interpret the history of the ideas, not merely the documents, of the formative age. I have spent nearly twenty-five years in what must be regarded as methodological and preparatory studies.

First through then-established methods and conceptions I pursued the same labor to which I now return: a history of Judaism in late antiquity. After a decade I recognized that these methods and conceptions ignored the entire critical agenda of the humanities from the Enlightenment forward. The critical program had been defined by rejection of that gullibility and credulous ignorance that, until Voltaire on the one side and the critical-historical scholars of biblical, classical, and medieval history on the other, had prevailed. Accordingly, the bulk of historical inquiry in "Talmudic history" was made up of citations of "facts" allegedly provided by texts that in fact no one had subject to sustained critical analysis. The narrative consisted of stories told in these same uncriticized texts. As a result, it seemed to me the first task was to seek a definition for the actual status of each of the documents viewed whole and complete.

This I did through my effort to define the Mishnah, the Tosefta, the Talmud of the Land of Israel, and a principal midrash composition, Leviticus Rabbah. I now move from the work of defining the sources and explaining their historical and conceptual character to a new labor entirely. It is to make use of these same sources to define and deal with those historical problems that, in my view, the sources permit us to address.

In so doing, in parts of the journey I walk once again that path of exploration laid forth in that vast heritage of learning I deem trivial. Others have worked on some of the topics at hand, for example, the Messiah. Because of the results of a quarter century of reading the sources as whole documents, one by one, asking about the character and viewpoint of each, I frame my steps differently from my predecessors, even when walking along the same road.

But the fact remains that, for the first time, I take up some questions of general interest, no longer insisting on the focus on problems of method and literary analysis. So the former studies -- Method and Meaning in Ancient Judaism and Formative Judaism -- centered on issues of method and the description, analysis, and interpretation of specific documents. Here, by contrast, I deal with results of methods I have worked out -- the outcome: the trends, characteristics, historical results. I believe we may begin to describe as a historical exercise the formation of a system of world-view and way of life of a distinct social group, the Talmudic rabbis and the social world addressed by them.

Clearly, my labor of literary study will reach completion only in the confrontation with the last of the documents of the formative age, the Talmud of Babylonia. But I believe that even now we can and should seek some concrete results. These of course will attain greater definition when the final chapter in the work has reached conclusion.

None of these papers has been printed elsewhere.

It remains to pay my tribute to the dear friends to whom this book is dedicated, Aaron and Elinor Ross Diamond. My family and I met the Diamonds on our tour of Papua New Guinea in the summer of 1983. We share with them an intense curiosity about everything. My path led to Port Moresby and the Sepik because I wanted to learn about the world before, other than, our own; I mean, a world before the West and modernization had made their marks. I had the notion that I could yet see in that remote and unsettling island-continent what I could not find at home. The Diamonds came en route from their journey to see the solar eclipse in Indonesia. Their eyes were on the stars, ours on ourselves and our experience before our own day. When we bumped into one another in Port Moresby, we discovered life-long friends, people whose hearts and minds had already joined. In the end, the Diamonds did see the eclipse. For our part, we found only the banal truth that our very presence is a mark that the West has arrived, cameras, tourists' gripes, and all. I learned more about humanity from the Diamonds than from the trip on which we met; this is my modest gift of thanks.

J.N.

Providence, Rhode Island
25 Tishre 5744
October 2, 1983

Part One

POLITICAL CRISIS, RELIGIOUS RESPONSE

Chapter One

STABLE SYMBOLS IN A SHIFTING SOCIETY:
THE DELUSION OF THE MONOLITHIC GENTILE IN DOCUMENTS OF
LATE FOURTH-CENTURY JUDAISM

When we examine the principal symbols of that form of Judaism represented by the writings of rabbis from the first century through the sixth, we of course find development and change as we move from one document to the next in line. The symbol of "Torah," for example, stands for some few things at the outset, and many more things at the end, of the formation of the rabbinic canon. The figure of the messiah also serves in more than a few ways. That fact hardly presents surprises. For in an age of change, over many hundreds of years, it is quite natural for people to make diverse and creative use of inherited modes of symbolization of the world. Accordingly, the stability of symbols -- the repeated reference over a long period of time to a severely limited repertoire -- masks the creative and original use of those symbols in response to the requirements of an ever-changing social world.

What demands attention is the opposite, the failure of people to reimagine a symbol that no longer corresponds to, or conveys, perceived reality. When, to be specific, people continue to speak in the same language about something that has in fact produced drastic change, we must ask why. For reason suggests symbols serve to construct an imaginary world that, for the structure to serve, must in some way correspond to the world out there. When, therefore, a critical area of social experience undergoes vast trans-formation, the symbols also should undergo metamorphosis. The one thing that should change is the character of the symbols through which people portray in their minds what is going on in that world that their minds and imaginations propose to mediate and to interpret.

To jump ahead in the argument and introduce the problem at hand, I point out that the mode of symbolization of the outsider, perceived as a nation and great power equivalent to Israel, remained stable during that period that marked Israel's complete transformation from one thing to something else. At the outset of the period at hand, before A.D. 70, Israel in its land constituted a small political entity, a state, like many others of its time and place. It was subordinate to a great empire, but was a distinct and autonomous unit, a part of the political structure of that empire. It had working institutions of self-government and politics. At the end of the same period, by the seventh century, Israel in no way constituted a political entity. Such institutions of a political or juridical character that it had had, had lost the recognition and legitimacy formerly conferred upon them.

Moreover, when Israel looked outward, toward the world beyond its limits, the changes proved no less stunning. At the outset, Rome, and at the end, Rome, but what a different Rome! In the first three centuries, Rome was what it had always been, what its predecessors in the Middle East had always been: pagan, essentially benign toward Israel in its land. From the fourth century, Rome became something unprecedented: a kind of Israel and a kin to Israel, a knowledgable competitor, a powerful and canny enemy, a brother.

The modes by which the Jews, or, more to the point, the rabbis whose writings survive, proposed to symbolize the world had therefore to take up two contradictory worlds. On the one hand these "symbols of the stranger," of Israel's history and destiny, and of Israel's relationship to the outsider, dealt with a world in which Israel was like the outsider: a nation among nations, a political entity confronting another such entity, thus history among other histories. At the end, these symbols had to convey the reality of an Israel that was essentially different in genus from the outsider: no longer a nation in the sense in which other groups constituted a nation, no longer a political entity like others, no longer standing at the end of a history essentially consubstantial with the history of the nations.

What we shall see is the surprising fact that, so far as we are able to tell, the modes of political and social symbolization remained essentially stable in a world of change. More to the point, the outsider remained what he had always been, a (mere) pagan, part of a world demanding from Israel no effort whatsoever at differentiation. The "nations" were all alike, and Israel was still not essentially different from them all: consubstantial, thus judged by the same standards, but to be sure guiltless while the rest were guilty. What makes so puzzling the stability of the modes of symbolization of Israel and the nations, Israel's history and destiny, and the substance of Israel's doctrine, is a simple fact. In the interval, Christianity had not only come to full and diverse expression, it also had reached power.

In coming to power, Christianity drew upon essentially the same symbolic heritage to which Israel had long had access. To Christianity as much as to Judaism the pagan was a pagan, not differentiated; history began in Eden and led through Sinai to the end of time; the Messiah stood at the climax and goal of this world's history; revelation ("Torah") came from one God to unique Israel. True, for all forms of Christianity, the values assigned to the repertoire of symbols at hand hardly corresponded to those imputed by the Jews. But the symbols remained the same, and so Israel now resorted to what had become a shared symbolic system and structure to express its history and politics.

Under such circumstances, who would be surprised to learn that deep thought went into the revision of the available symbols, a restatement in such wise as to differentiate what had been treated as uniform, to redefine what had been grasped as settled? Surely the Christian, in the symbolic system of Judaism, should look like something other than the pagan, maybe worse but at least different. Certainly history as a mode of social symbolization should proceed on a somewhat different path from the one it had taken when the one God had not yet come to rule, when Israel's ancient Scriptures had not yet come to define the nature and destiny of humanity. Reckoning with the profound political changes at hand, we might imagine, should lead at least some profound thinkers to reconsider the symbolic system that had formerly prevailed or, at the very least, the nature and definition of symbols that had gone forward into the new age and remained vivid. After all, social change should generate symbol change, political change should make its mark upon the symbols of politics and society.

But if that is what reason dictates we should expect, it is not how things actually happened. As I shall point out, it would take the rabbis of the canon of Judaism nearly a millenium to take seriously the specific character and claims of Christianity and to begin to counter in a systematic way the concrete assertions of that religious tradition. Before the High Middle Ages, Judaism would have nothing to say about, let alone to, Christianity. More probative, Jewish thinkers would maintain the fantastic pretense that nothing important happened in either the first or the fourth century, that is, in either the supernatural or the political world at hand. As we shall now see, one important indicator of that fact is the unwillingness of the rabbinic exegetes of the fourth and early fifth centuries to concede that Christians were different from pagans. On the contrary, the rabbinic sources treat all pagans as essentially faceless, and Christianity not at all, except as part of that same blank wall of hostility to God (and, by the way, to Israel).

Before we proceed, we should take note of a parallel and still more striking case of a nation's incapacity to differentiate among outsiders, aliens, enemies. I refer to the case of Rome, which saw as uniform, as mere barbarians, all with the same policy and plan, what was in fact a vastly differentiated and diverse world of outsiders.

That fact is brilliantly expounded by Walter Goffart in his "Rome, Constantinople, and the Barbarians" (American Historical Review, 1981, 86:275-306), who points out how ancient authors in Rome followed the convention of "portraying the tribes of their time under anachronistic names drawn from Herodotus and Tacitus." Goffart comments, "Precisely because the barbarians were always there, never seeming to contemporary observers from the Mediterranean to acquire new characteristics more dangerous than those of the past, there is little reason to look among them for a clue to their startling career in the fifth and sixth centuries A.D." On the Roman side of the frontier, the terms of the encounter remained stable. More important, the term "barbarian" transformed the Roman Empire's neighbors "into a collectivity" (all quotes: p. 277). Consequently, the Romans tended to see all their enemies as essentially uniform and to assume all outsiders were enemies.

That fact is contrary to reality, for, as Goffart says (p. 279), "At no time in antiquity, early or late, was there a collective hostility of barbarians toward the empire or a collective purpose to tear it down." Goffart makes the case that Roman policy toward "the barbarians" failed to take account of the diversity of the challenges presented to the security of the Empire by diverse enemies. So he asks, "Why did the emperors respond more peacefully to barbarian attacks after 376 and 406 than their predecessors had in the third century?" Following his sequence of related questions, Goffart concludes, "The bond between such questions is that each one forces us to look elsewhere for answers than among the nonliterate barbarians." The answer (if I may state matters in a general way) lies in the capacity of the Romans' policy-makers to imagine things through the veil of language -- hence, symbols -- that obscured change.

Now we need hardly be surprised to find in the formative documents of Judaism an equivalent set of tendencies. Three prove most prominent: first, the repeated recourse to anachronism; second, the insistence that the world beyond was essentially undifferentiated; and third, the failure to take account, in the symbolization of the social world, of fundamental change.

To give examples of each tendency at the outset, the Mishnah, for its part, describes a political system for Israel in which the people are ruled by a king and high priest, in consultation with a sanhedrin. That quaint portrait, provided by Mishnah-tractate Sanhedrin, not only ignores the political institutions that did exist in the second century. It also evokes a political system that, in fact, never existed in Israelite history prior to its own time. For we cannot point to a single period in the political history of the Jewish nation in which the government consisted of an independent king, high priest, and sanhedrin, conducting affairs in the antiseptic separation of powers fantasized by the authors of the Mishnah-tractate. Indeed, it is probably an understatement to call the portrait a mere anachronism, but from the perspective of the second-century authors, that is what they presented.

The undifferentiation of the outside world may be conveyed in a simple fact. The entire earth outside of the Land of Israel in the Mishnah's law was held to suffer from contamination by corpses. Hence it was unclean with a severe mode of uncleanness, inaccessible to the holy and life-sustaining processes of the cult. If an Israelite artist were asked to paint a wall-portrait of the world beyond the Land, he would paint the entire wall white, the color of death. The outside world, in the imagination of the Mishnah's law, was the realm of death. Among corpses, how are we to make distinctions?

The failure of symbols to respond to changes in the very social world that they are meant to convey and express, as is clear, forms the focus of what is to come. For this purpose, we speak of modes of symbolization of the outside world, which is to say, means of differentiation between society and the stranger, ways in which people reckon with "the other" in all the manifold ways in which "the other" makes an impact upon "us."

For the present purpose, we take up the most complex "other" with which Jewish thinkers of late antiquity had to contend, namely, the outsider who was not depraved, not barbarian, not pagan, not beyond the realm of the Torah -- but who also was not inside. I refer, of course, to the Christians in their many and rich forms. Obviously, we cannot ask the sages of the rabbinic literature to tell us the difference between Arius and Athanasius, or between Marcion and Orthodox Christianity. But we must wonder whether they knew that a Christian was not some form of pagan and, if they did, how they expressed the difference. For the present purpose, we want to ask not about scattered sayings. Everyone knows, for instance, that to the first-century authority, Tarfon is attributed the angry observation that there were people around who knew the truth of the Torah but rejected it:

> The books of the Evangelists and the books of the minim they do not save from
> a fire [on the Sabbath]. They are allowed to burn up where they are, they and
> [even] the references to the Divine Name that are in them... Said R. Tarfon,
> "May I bury my sons if such things come into my hands and I do not burn them,
> and even the references to the Divine Name which are in them. And if
> someone was running after me, I should escape into a temple of idolatry, but I

should not go into their houses of worship. For idolators do not recognize the Divinity in denying him, but these recognize the Divinity and deny him. About them Scripture states, "Behind the door and the doorpost you have set your symbol for deserting me, you have uncovered your bed' (Is. 57:8)." (Tosefta Shabbat 13:5)

This statement has long persuaded scholars that the rabbinic authority recognized the difference between pagans and those minim under discussion, reasonably assumed to be Christian. I see no reason to differ from the established consensus.

Yet it does not materially advance our inquiry. For we want to know about the collective and large-scale symbols, to which people repeatedly resorted when they wished to speak about the outsider in general or the Christian in particular. For that purpose the well-known passage at hand serves not at all. Rather, we need to turn to passages that speak collectively, thus for the consensus of the community of sages and as part of its canon. We want to identify not merely explicit sayings, but, for the purpose of this discussion, symbols and (more important) modes of symbolization. That is, we want to find out how people speak of "the outsider" and "the Christian" when they do not wish to refer in a limited way but rather to speak in evocative and powerful symbols. What are these symbols, that is, things that speak of something in terms of something else and serve powerfully to evoke emotion and strong feeling in so doing?

Before proceeding to identify an appropriate symbol and to examine its use, let me restate the argument at hand. I want to know how rabbis of the formative centuries of Judaism symbolized the world beyond, how they spoke about "the other." We know that they saw the whole world as "pagan," so that deep in the rhetorical structures of their language and mode of thought lay embedded the distinction between "Israel" and "everybody else." That is not new or surprising. But how, in particular, did these same thinkers express and convey something more subtle, namely, the difference among outsiders, as that difference emerged among people who were not Israel but also not pagan? And, as I have made clear, we wish to identify how in symbolic discourse in particular the formative minds framed issues and phrased matters. For the issue is not what people thought in general but how they cast their thoughts in particular into evocative symbols.

The probative evidence derives from an example of thinking at its most symbolic, that is to say, passages in which discourse repeatedly avoids saying things straight out but rather turns to language and images meant to say something in terms of something else. We have further to identify symbols of the outsider -- and of differentiation among outsiders -- which occur over and over again, that is to say, symbols that shout their messages so loud and clear that further exposition proves unnecessary. At the same time, we seek examples of discourse at its most symbolic, so that we may see how people were framing one thing in terms of something else.

We further want to find documents that address an age of radical social change, so that we may assess the stability or the resilience of a symbolic system put to the test. And, finally, we require a symbolic statement cast in such a way that we may compare how diverse groups, at different times, made use of the same symbols.

These criteria are met by those passages of Leviticus Rabbah that deal with the course of human history and, in particular, that portray in powerful symbols the past and present destiny of the great empires of the world. The message of the symbolization of the nations comes through in the choice of animals selected to stand for the several empires under discussion. The beasts of Daniel's vision serve. Leviticus Rabbah came to closure, it is generally agreed, around A.D. 400, that is, approximately a century after the Roman Empire in the east had begun to become Christian, and half a century after the last attempt to rebuild the Temple in Jerusalem had failed -- a tumultuous age indeed. Finally, we even have evidence of other ways, besides those we shall review, of making use of these same symbols. Accordingly, we have the chance to see how distinctive and striking are the ways in which, in the text at hand, the symbols of animals that stand for the four successive empires of humanity and point towards the messianic time, serve for the framers' message.

Before we turn to the passage itself, let us turn aside and take up the task of describing the age, that is, the events of the fourth century and the way in which, in rabbinic documents of that time and afterward, these events make their impact.

For nearly everyone in the Roman world the most important events of the fourth and fifth centuries, the period in which the Talmud of the Land of Israel and collections of exegeses such as Leviticus Rabbah were coming into being, were, first, the legalization of Christianity, followed very rapidly, second, by the adoption of Christianity as the state's most favored religion, and, third, by the delegitimization of paganism and systematic degradation of Judaism. The astonishing advent of legitimacy and even power provoked Christian intellectuals to rewrite Christian and world history, and work out theology as a reflection on this new polity and its meaning in the unfolding of human history. A new commonwealth was coming into being, taking over the old and reshaping it for the new age. In 312 Constantine achieved power in the West. In 323 he took the government of the entire Roman empire into his own hands. He promulgated the edict of Milan in 313, whereby Christianity attained the status of toleration. Christians and all others were given "the free power to follow the religion of their choice." In the next decade Christianity became the most favored religion. Converts from Judaism were protected and could not be punished by Jews. Christians were freed of the obligation to perform pagan sacrifices. Priests were exempted from certain taxes. Sunday became an obligatory day of rest. Celibacy was permitted. From 324 onward Constantine ceased to maintain a formal impartiality, now intervening in the affairs of the Church, settling quarrels among believers, and calling the Church Council at Nicaea (325) to settle issues of the faith. He was baptized only on the eve of his death in 337. Over the next century the pagan cults were destroyed, their priests deprived of support, their intellectuals bereft of standing.

So far as the Jews of the Land of Israel were concerned, not much changed at the Milvian Bridge in 312, when Constantine conquered in the sign of Christ. The sages' writings nowhere refer explicitly to that event. They scarcely gave testimony to its consequences for the Jews, and continued to harp upon prohibited relationships with "pagans" in general, as though nothing had changed from the third century to the fourth and fifth. Legal changes affecting the Jews under Constantine's rule indeed were not substantial. Jews could not proselytize; they could not circumcise slaves when they bought them; Jews could not punish other Jews who became Christians. Jews, finally, were required to serve on municipal councils wherever they lived, an onerous task involving responsibility for collecting taxes. But those who served synagogues, patriarchs, and priests were still exempted from civil and personal obligations. In the reign of Constantius III (337-361), further laws aimed at separating Jews from Christians were enacted, in 339 in the Canons of Elvira. These forbade intermarriage between Jews and Christians, further protected converts, and forbade Jews to hold slaves of Christian or other gentile origin.

The reversion to paganism on the part of the emperor Julian, ca. 360, involved a measure of favor to Jews and Judaism. To embarrass Christianity, he permitted the rebuilding of the Temple at Jerusalem, but he died before much progress could be made. In the aftermath of the fiasco of Julian's reversion to paganism, the Christians, returning to power, determined to make certain such a calamity would never recur. Accordingly over the next century they undertook a sustained attack on institutions and personnel of paganism in all its expressions. The long-term and systematic effort in time overspread Judaism as well. From the accession of Theodosius II in 383 to the death of his son, Arcadius in 408, Judaism came under attack. In the earlier part of the fifth century, Jews' rights and the standing of their corporate communities were substantially affected. The patriarchate of the Jews of the Land of Israel, the ethnarch and his administration, was abolished. So from the turn of the fifth century, the government policy was meant to isolate Jews, lower their status, and suppress their agencies of self-rule.

Laws against intermarriage posed no problem to the Jews. The ones limiting proselytism and those protecting converts from Judaism, did not affect many people. But the edicts that reduced Jews to second-class citizenship did matter. They were not to hold public office, but still had to sit on city councils responsible for the payment of taxes. Later, they were removed from the councils, though still obligated, of course, for taxes. Between 404 and 438 Jews were forbidden to hold office in the civil service, represent cities, serve in the army or at the bar, and they ultimately were evicted from every public office. In all, the later fourth and fifth centuries for Israel in its land marked a time of significant change. Once a mere competing faith, Christianity now became paramount. The period from Julian's fall onward, moreover, presented to Israel problems of a profoundly religious character. To these we now turn.

There were five events of fundamental importance for the history of Judaism in the fourth and fifth centuries. All of them except for the last were well known in their day. These were as follows: (1) the conversion of Constantine; (2) the fiasco of Julian's plan to rebuild the Temple of Jerusalem; (3) the depaganization of the Roman empire, a program of attacks on pagan temples and, along the way, synagogues; (4) the Christianization of the majority of the population of Palestine; and (5) the creation of the Talmud of the Land of Israel and of compositions of Scriptural exegeses. The Talmud and the exegetical compilations came into begin in an age of crisis, high hope, and then disaster. Vast numbers of Jews now found chimerical the messianic expectation, as they had framed it around Julian's plan to rebuild the Temple. So it was a time of boundless expectations followed by bottomless despair.

Let us briefly review from the present perspective the four events that framed the setting for the fifth, starting with Constantine's conversion. The first point is that we do not know how Jews responded to Constantine's establishment of Christianity as the most favored religion. But in the Land of Israel itself, his works were well known, since he and his mother purchased many sites believed connected with Israel's sacred history and built churches and shrines at them. They rewrote the map of the Land of Israel. Every time they handled a coin, moreover, Jews had to recognize that something of fundamental importance had shifted, for the old pagan images were blotted out as Christian symbols took their place -- public events indeed!

A move of the empire from reverence for Zeus to adoration of Mithra meant nothing; paganism was what it was, lacking all differentiation in the Jewish eye. As I have stressed, Christianity was something else. It was different. It was like Judaism. Christians read the Torah and claimed to declare its meaning. Accordingly, the trend of sages' speculation cannot have avoided the issue of the place, within the Torah's messianic pattern, of the remarkable turn in world history represented by the triumph of Christianity. Since the Christians vociferously celebrated confirmation of their faith in Christ's messiahship and, at the moment, Jews were hardly prepared to concur, it falls surely within known patterns for us to suppose that Constantine's conversion would have been identified with some dark moment to prefigure the dawning of the messianic age.

Second, if people were then looking for a brief dawn, the emperor Julian's plan to rebuild the ruined Temple in Jerusalem must have dazzled their eyes. For while Constantine surely raised the messianic question, for a brief hour Emperor Julian appeared decisively to answer it. In 361 the now-pagan Julian gave permission to rebuild the Temple. Work briefly got underway, but stopped because of an earthquake. The intention of Julian's plan was quite explicit. Julian had had in mind to falsify the prophecy of Jesus that "not one stone of the temple would be left upon another." We may take for granted that, since Christ's prophecy had not been proven false, many surely concluded that it indeed had now been shown true. We do not know that Jews in numbers then drew the conclusion that, after all, Jesus really was the Christ. Many Christians said so. But in the next half century, Palestine gained a Christian majority. Christians were not slow to claim their faith had been proved right. We need not speculate on the depth of disappointment felt by those Jews who had hoped that the project would come to fruition and herald, instead of the Christian one, the Messiah they awaited.

Third, the last pagan emperor's threat to Christianity made urgent the delegitimization of paganism. In the formation of a new and aggressive policy toward outsiders, Judaism, too, was caught in the net. To be sure, Jews were to be protected but degraded. But the sword unsheathed against the pagan cult-places, if sharp, was untutored. It was not capable of discriminating among non-Christian centers of divine service. Nor could those who wielded it, zealots of the faith in church and street, have been expected to. The now-Christian Roman government protected synagogues and punished those who damaged them. Its policy was to extirpate paganism but protect a degraded Judaism. But the faithful of the church had their own ideas. The assault against pagan temples spilled over into an ongoing program of attacking synagogue property.

Still worse from the Jews' viewpoint, a phenomenon lacking much precedent over the antecedent thousand years now came into view: random attacks on Jews by reason of their faith, as distinct from organized struggles among contending and equal forces, Jewish and other mobs. The long-established Roman tradition of toleration of Judaism and of Jews, extending back to the time of Julius Caesar and applying both in law and in custom, now drew to a close. A new fact, at this time lacking all basis in custom and in the policy of state and Church alike, faced Jews: physical insecurity in their own villages and towns. So Jews' synagogues and their homes housed the same thing, which was to be eradicated: Judaism. A mark of exceptional piety came to consist in violence against Jews' holy places, their property and persons. Coming in the aftermath of the triumph of Christianity on the one side, and the decisive disproof of the Jews' hope for the rebuilding of the Temple on the other, was the hitherto-unimagined war against the Jews. In the last third of the fourth century and the beginning of the fifth, this war raised once again those questions about the meaning and end of history that Constantine, at the beginning of the age at hand, had forced upon Israel's consciousness.

Fourth, at this time there seems to have been a sharp rise in the numbers of Christians in the Holy Land. Christian refugees from the West accounted for part of the growth. But we have some stories about how Jews converted as well. The number of Christian towns and villages dramatically increased. If Jews did convert in sizeable numbers, then we should have to point to the events of the preceding decades as ample validation in their eyes for the Christian interpretation of history. Jews had waited nearly three hundred years, from the destruction in 70 to the promise of Julian. Instead of being falsified, Jesus' prophecy had been validated. No stone had been left on stone in the Temple, not after 70, not after 361, just as Jesus had said. Instead of a rebuilt temple, the Jews looked out on a world in which now even their synagogues came under threat and, along with them, their own homes and persons. What could be more ample proof of the truth of the Christians' claim than the worldly triumph of their Church? Resisted for so long, that claim called into question, as in the time of Bar Kokhba, whether it was worth waiting any longer for a messiah that had not come when he was most needed. With followers proclaiming the messiah who _had_ come now possessing the world, the question could hardly be avoided.

Now that we understand the context, we appreciate the issues at hand. What has happened is a world-historical change, one that could not be absorbed into Israel's available system of theories on the outsiders, in general, and the meaning of the history of the great empires, in particular. The Christian empire was fundamentally different from its predecessor in two ways. First, it shared with Israel reverence for exactly the same Holy Scriptures on which Jewry based its existence. So it was no longer a wholly other, entirely alien empire that ruled over the horizon. It was now a monotheist, formerly persecuted, biblical empire, not awfully different from Israel in its basic convictions about all important matters of time and eternity. And it was near at hand and inter-ested. Second, established policies of more than a half a millenium, from the time of the

Maccabees' alliance with Rome to the start of the fourth century, now gave way. Tolerance of Judaism and an accomodation with the Jews in their Land -- disrupted only by the Jews' own violation of the terms of the agreement in 70 and 132 -- now no longer governed. Instead, we find intolerance of Judaism and persecution of Jews through attacks on their persons and property.

Accordingly, we must ask how documents of the age at hand addressed the issue of, first the course of human events, and second, the character of Rome in particular. To take up that issue, we turn to the apocalyptic passage of Scripture that served to define the images at hand, Daniel's vision of the nations in terms of various animals. The first use of these symbols shows us a way not taken, that is, how rabbis not interested in the issues at hand -- probably living a century or more before world-historical change made an impact on the consciousness of the sages' community -- treated these images. Only then we shall turn to the treatment of the animal-symbols in the period at hand.

We take up Tosefta's treatment of the apocalyptic vision of Daniel and find that history happens in what takes place in the sages debates.

T. Miqvaot 7:11

A. A cow which drank purification-water, and which one slaughtered within twenty-four hours --

B. This was a case, and R. Yose the Galilean did declare it clean, and R. Aqiba did declare it unclean.

C. R. Tarfon supported R. Yose the Galilean. R. Simeon ben Nanos supported R. Aqiba.

D. R. Simeon b. Nanos dismissed [the arguments of] R. Tarfon. R. Yose the Galilean dismissed [the arguments of] R. Simeon b. Nanos.

E. R. Aqiba dismissed [the arguments of] R. Yose the Galilean.

F. After a time, he [Yose] found an answer for him [Aqiba].

G. He said to him, "Am I able to reverse myself?"

H. He said to him, "Not anyone [may reverse himself], but you [may do so], for you are Yose the Galilean."

I. [He said to him,] "I shall say to you: Lo, Scripture states, <u>And they shall be kept for the congregation of the people of Israel for the water for impurity</u> (Num. 19:9).

J. "Just so long as they are kept, lo, they are water for impurity -- but not after a cow has drunk them."

K. This was a case, and thirty-two elders voted in Lud and declared it clean.

L. At that time R. Tarfon recited this verse:

M. "<u>I saw the ram goring westward and northward and southward, and all the animals were unable to stand against it, and none afforded protection from its power, and it did just as it liked and grew great</u> (Dan. 8:4) --

N. "[This is] R. Aqiba.

O. "'<u>As I was considering, behold, a he-goat came from the west across the face of the whole earth, without touching the ground; and the goat had a conspicuous horn between his eyes.</u>

P.   "'He came to the ram with the two horns, which I had seen standing on the bank of the river, and he ran at him in his mighty wrath. I saw him come close to the ram, and he was enraged against him and struck the ram and broke his two horns' -- this is R. Aqiba and R. Simeon b. Nanos.

Q.   "'And the ram had no power to stand before him' -- this is R. Aqiba.

R.   "'But he cast him down to the ground and trampled upon him' -- this is R. Yose the Galilena.

S.   "'And there was no one who could rescue the ram from his power' -- these are the thirty-two elders who voted in Lud and declared it clean.'"

We shall see the same passage in its own context. I cite it here only to underline the contrast between the usage at hand and the one we find in the late fourth or early fifth century composition, Leviticus Rabbah. What we see here is how sages absorb events into their system of classification. So it is sages that make history through the thoughts they think and the rules they lay down. In such a context, we find no interest either in the outsiders and their powers, or in the history of the empires of the world, or, all the more so, in redemption and the messianic fulfillment of time.

What is the alternative to the use of the sort of symbols just now examined? Let us turn immediately to the relevant passages of Leviticus Rabbah:

XIII:V

1.   A.   Said R. Ishmael b. R. Nehemiah, "All the prophets foresaw what the pagan kingdoms would do [to Israel].

     B.   "The first man foresaw what the pagan kingdoms would do [to Israel].

     C.   "That is in line with the following verse of Scripture: 'A river flowed out of Eden [to water the garden, and there it divided and became four rivers]' (Gen. 2:10). [The four rivers stand for the four kingdoms, Babylonia, Media, Greece, and Rome]."

2.   A.   R. Tanhuma said it, [and] R. Menahema [in the name of] R. Joshua b. Levi: "The Holy One, blessed be he, will give the cup of reeling to the nations of the world to drink in the world to come.

     B.   "That is in line with the following verse of Scripture: 'A river flowed out of Eden' (Gen 2:10), the place from which justice [DYN] goes forth."

3.   A.   "[There it divided] and became four rivers" (Gen 2:10) -- this refers to the four kingdoms.

     B.   "The name of the first is Pishon (PSWN); [it is the one which flows around the whole land of Havilah, where there is gold; and the gold of that land is good; bdellium and onyx stone are there]" (Gen. 2:11-12).

     C.   This refers to Babylonia, on account [of the reference to Babylonia in the following verse:] "And their [the Babylonians'] horsemen spread themselves (PSW)" (Hab. 1:8).

     D.   [It is further] on account of [Nebuchadnezzar's being] a dwarf, shorter than ordinary men by a handbreadth.

E. "[It is the one which flows around the whole land of Havilah" (Gen. 2:11).

F. "This [reference to the river's flowing around the whole land] speaks of Nebuchadnezzar, the wicked man, who came up and surrounded the entire Land of Israel, which places its hope in the Holy One, blessed be he.

G. That is in line with the following verse of Scripture: "Hope in God, for I shall again praise him" (Ps. 42:5).

H. "Where there is gold" (Gen. 2:11) -- this refers to the words of Torah, "which are more to be desired than gold, more than much fine gold" (Ps. 19:11).

I. "And the gold of that land is good" (Gen. 2:12).

J. This teaches that there is no Torah like the Torah that is taught in the Land of Israel, and there is no wisdom like the wisdom that is taught in the Land of Israel.

K. Bdellium and onyx stone are there" (Gen. 2:12) -- Scripture, Mishnah, Talmud, and lore.

4. A. "The name of the second river is Gihon; [it is the one which flows around the whole land of Cush]" (Gen. 2:13).

B. This refers to Media, which produced Haman, that wicked man, who spit out venom like a serpent.

C. It is on account of the verse: "On your belly will you go" (Gen. 3:14).

D. "It is the one which flows around the whole land of Cush" (Gen. 2:13).

E. [We know that this refers to Media, because it is said:] "Who rules from India to Cush" (Est. 1:1).

5. A. "And the name of the third river is Tigris (HDQL), [which flows east of Assyria] (Gen. 2:14).

B. This refers to Greece [Syria], which was sharp (HD) and speedy (QL) in making its decrees, saying to Israel, "Write on the horn of an ox that you have no portion in the God of Israel."

C. "Which flows east (QDMT) of Assyria" (Gen. 2:14).

D. Said R. Huna, "In three aspects the kingdom of Greece was in advance (QDMH) of the present evil kingdom [Rome]: in respect to ship-building, the arrangement of camp vigils, and language."

E. Said R. Huna, "Any and every kingdom may be called 'Assyria' (ashur), on account of all of their making themselves powerful at Israel's expense."

F. Said R. Yose b. R. Hanina, "Any and every kingdom may be called Nineveh (NNWH), on account of their adorning (NWY) themselves at Israel's expense."

G. Said R. Yose b. R. Hanina, "Any and every kingdom may be called Egypt (MSRYM), on account of their oppressing (MSYRYM) Israel."

6. A. "And the fourth river is the Euphrates (PRT)" (Gen. 2:14).

B. This refers to Edom [Rome], since it was fruitful (PRT), and multiplied through the prayer of the elder [Isaac at Gen. 27:39].

C. Another interpretation: "It was because it was fruitful and multiplied, and so cramped his world.

D.   Another explanation: Because it was fruitful and multiplied and cramped his son.

E.   Another explanation: Because it was fruitful and multiplied and cramped his house.

F.   Another explanation: "Parat" -- because in the end, "I am going to exact a penalty from it (PR^C)."

G.   That is in line with the following verse of Scripture: "I have trodden (PWRH) the winepress alone" (Is. 63:3).

7. A.   [Gen. R. 42:2:] Abraham foresaw what the evil kingdoms would do [to Israel].

B.   "[As the sun was going down,] a deep sleep fell on Abraham; and lo, a dread and great darkness fell upon him]" (Gen. 15:12).

C.   "Dread" ('YMH) refers to Babylonia, on account of the statement, "Then Nebuchadnezzer was full of fury (HMH)" (Dan. 3:19).

D.   "Darkness" refers to Media, which brought darkness to Israel through its decrees: "to destroy, to slay, and to wipe out all the Jews" (Est. 7:4).

E.   "Great" refers to Greece.

F.   Said R. Judah b. R. Simon, "The verse teaches that the kingdom of Greece set up one hundred twenty-seven governors, one hundred and twenty-seven hyparchs and one hundred twenty-seven commanders."

G.   And rabbis say, "They were sixty in each category."

H.   R. Berekhiah and R. Hanan in support of this position taken by rabbis: "'Who led you through the great terrible wilderness, with its fiery serpents and scorpions and thirsty ground where there was no water]' (Deut. 8:15).

I.   "Just as the scorpion produces eggs by sixties, so the kingdom of Greece would set up its administration in groups of sixty."

J.   "Fell on him" (Gen. 15:12).

K.   This refers to Edom, on account of the following verse: "The earth quakes at the noise of their [Edom's] fall" (Jer. 49:21).

L.   There are those who reverse matters.

M.   "Fear" refers to Edom, on account of the following verse: "And this I saw, a fourth beast, fearful, and terrible" (Dan. 7:7).

M.   "Darkness" refers to Greece, which brought gloom through its decrees. For they said to Israel, "Write on the horn of an ox that you have no portion in the God of Israel."

O.   "Great" refers to Media, on account of the verse: "King Ahasuerus made Haman [the Median] great" (Est. 3:1).

P.   "Fell on him" refers to Babylonia, on account of the following verse: "Fallen, fallen is Babylonia" (Is. 21:9).

8. A.   Daniel foresaw what the evil kingdoms would do [to Israel].

B.   "Daniel said, I saw in my vision by night, and behold, the four winds of heaven were stirring up the great sea. And four great beasts came up out of the sea, [different from one another. The first was like a lion and had eagles' wings. Then as I looked, its wings were plucked off... And behold, another beast, a second one, like a bear.... After this I looked, and lo, another, like a leopard.... After this I saw in the night visions, and behold, a fourth beast, terrible and dreadful and exceedingly strong; and it had great iron teeth]" (Dan. 7:3-7).

C. If you enjoy sufficient merit, it will emerge from the sea, but if not, it will come out of the forest.

D. The animal that comes up from the sea is not violent, but the one that comes up out of the forest is violent.

E. Along these same lines: "The boar out of the wood ravages it" (Ps. 80:14).

F. If you enjoy sufficient merit, it will come from the river, and if not, from the forest.

G. The animal that comes up from the river is not violent, but the one that comes up out of the forest is violent.

H. "Different from one another" (Dan. 7:3).

I. Differing from [hating] one another.

J. This teaches that every nation that rules in the world hates Israel and reduces them to slavery.

K. "The first was like a lion [and had eagles' wings]" (Dan. 7:4).

L. This refers to Babylonia.

M. Jeremiah saw [Babylonia] as a lion. Then he went and saw it as an eagle.

N. He saw it as a lion: "A lion has come up from his thicket" (Jer. 4:7).

O. And [as an eagle:] "Behold, he shall come up and swoop down as the eagle" (Jer. 49:22).

P. People said to Daniel, "What do you see?"

Q. He said to them, "I see the face like that of a lion and wings like those of an eagle: 'The first was like a lion and had eagles' wings. Then, as I looked, its wings were plucked off, and it was lifted up from the ground [and made to stand upon two feet like a man and the heart of a man was given to it]' (Dan. 7:4).

R. R. Eleazar and R. Ishmael b. R. Nehemiah:

S. R. Eleazar said, "While the entire lion was smitten, its heart was not smitten.

T. "That is in line with the following statement: 'And the heart of a man was given to it' (Dan. 7:4)."

U. And R. Ishmael b. R. Nehemiah said, "Even its heart was smitten, for it is written, 'Let his heart be changed from a man's' (Dan. 4:17).

X. "And behold, another beast, a second one, like a bear. [It was raised up one side; it had three ribs in its mouth between its teeth, and it was told, Arise, devour much flesh]" (Dan. 7:5).

Y. This refers to Media.

Z. Said R. Yohanan, "It is like a bear."

AA. It is written, "similar to a wolf" (DB); thus, "And a wolf was there."

BB. That is in accord with the view of R. Yohanan, for R.Yohanan said, "'Therefore a lion out of the forest [slays them]' (Jer. 5:6) -- this refers to Babylonia.

CC. "'A wolf of the deserts spoils them' (Jer. 5:6) refers to Media.

DD. "'A leopard watches over their cities' (Jer. 5:6) refers to Greece.

EE. "'Whoever goes out from them will be savaged' (Jer. 5:6) refers to Edom.

FF. "Why so? 'Because their transgressions are many, and their backslidings still more' (Jer. 5:6)."

GG. "After this, I looked, and lo, another, like a leopard [with four wings of a bird on its back; and the beast had four heads; and dominion was given to it]" (Dan. 7:6).

HH. This [leopard] refers to Greece, which persisted impudently in making harsh decrees, saying to Israel, "Write on the horn of an ox that you have no share in the God of Israel."

II. "After this I saw in the night visions, and behold, a fourth beast, terrible and dreadful and exceedingly strong; [and it had great iron teeth; it devoured and broke in pieces and stamped the residue with its feet. It was different from all the beasts that were before it; and it had ten horns]" (Dan. 7:7).

JJ. This refers to Edom [Rome].

KK. Daniel saw the first three visions on one night, and this one he saw on another night. Now why was that the case?

LL. R. Yohanan and R. Simeon b. Laqish:

MM. R. Yohanan said, "It is because the fourth beast weighed as much as the first three."

NN. And R. Simeon b. Laqish said, "It outweighed them."

OO. R. Yohanan objected to R. Simeon b. Laqish, "'Prophesy, therefore, son of man, clap your hands [and let the sword come down twice; yea, thrice. The sword for those to be slain; it is the sword for the great slaughter, which encompasses them]' (Ez. 21:14-15). [So the single sword of Rome weighs against the three others]."

PP. And R. Simeon b. Laqish, how does he interpret the same passage? He notes that [the threefold sword] is doubled (Ez. 21:14), [thus outweighs the three swords, equally twice their strength].

9. A. Moses foresaw what the evil kingdoms would do [to Israel].

B. "The camel, rock badger, and hare" (Deut. 14:7). [Compare: "Nevertheless, among those that chew the cud or part the hoof, you shall not eat these: the camel, because it chews the cud but does not part the hoof, is unclean to you. The rock badger, because it chews the cud but does not part the hoof, is unclean to you. And the hare, because it chews the cud but does not part the hoof, is unclean to you, and the pig, because it parts the hoof and is cloven-footed, but does not chew the cud, is unclean to you" (Lev. 11:4-8).]

C. The camel (GML) refers to Babylonia, [in line with the following verse of Scripture: "O daughter of Babylonia, you who are to be devastated! Happy will be he who requites (GML) you, with what you have done to us" (Ps. 147:8).

D. "The rock badger" (Deut. 14:7) -- this refers to Media.

E. Rabbis and R. Judah b. R. Simon.

F.   Rabbis say, "Just as the rock badger exhibits traits of uncleanness and traits of cleanness, so the kingdom of Media produced both a righteous man and a wicked one."

G.   Said R. Judah b. R. Simon, "The last Darius was Esther's son. He was clean on his mother's side and unclean on his father's side."

H.   "The hare" (Deut 14:7) -- this refers to Greece. The mother of King Ptolemy was named "Hare" [in Greek: lagos].

I.   "The pig" (Deut. 14:7) -- this refers to Edom [Rome].

J.   Moses made mention of the first three in a single verse and the final one in a verse by itself [(Deut. 14:7, 8)]. Why so?

K.   R. Yohanan and R. Simeon b. Laqish.

L.   R. Yohanan said, "It is because [the pig] is equivalent to the other three."

M.   And R. Simeon b. Laqish said, "It is because it outweighs them."

N.   R. Yohanan objected to R. Simeon b. Laqish, "'Prophesy, therefore, son of man, clap your hands [and let the sword come down twice, yea thrice]' (Ez. 21:14)."

O.   And how does R. Simeon b. Laqish interpret the same passage? He notes that [the threefold sword] is doubled (Ez. 21:14).

10. A.   [Gen. R. 65:1:] R. Phineas and R. Hilqiah in the name of R. Simon: "Among all the prophets, only two of them revealed [the true evil of Rome], Assaf and Moses.

B.   "Assaf said, 'The pig out of the wood ravages it' (Ps. 80:14).

C.   "Moses said, 'And the pig, [because it parts the hoof and is cloven-footed but does not chew the cud]' (Lev. 11:7).

D.   "Why is [Rome] compared to a pig?

E.   "It is to teach you the following: Just as, when a pig crouches and produces its hooves, it is as if to say, 'See how I am clean [since I have a cloven hoof],' so this evil kingdom takes pride, seizes by violence, and steals, and then gives the appearance of establishing a tribunal for justice."

F.   There was the case of a ruler in Caesarea, who put thieves, adulterers, and sorcerers to death, while at the same time telling his counsellor, "That same man [I] did all these three things on a single night."

11. A.   Another interpretation: "The camel" (Lev. 11:4).

B.   This refers to Babylonia.

C.   "Because it chews the cud (M^CLH GRH) [but does not part the hoof]" (Lev. 11:4).

D.   For it brings forth praises [with its throat (MQLS)] of the Holy One, blessed be he. [The Hebrew words for "chew the cud" -- bring up cud -- are now understood to mean "give praise." GRH is connected with GRWN, throat, hence, "bring forth [sounds of praise through] the throat."

E.   R. Berekhiah and R. Helbo in the name of R. Ishmael b. R. Nahman: "Whatever [praise of God] David [in writing a psalm] treated singly [item by item], that wicked man [Nebuchadnezzar] lumped together in a single verse.

F.   "'Now I, Nebuchadnezzar, praise and extol and honor the King of heaven, for all his works are right and his ways are just, and those who walk in pride he is able to abase' (Dan. 4:37).

G.   "'Praise' -- 'O Jerusalem, praise the Lord' (Ps. 147:12).

H.   "'Extol' -- 'I shall extol you, O Lord, for you have brought me low' (Ps. 30:2).

I.   "'Honor the king of heaven' -- 'The Lord reigns, let the peoples tremble! He sits enthroned upon the cherubim, let the earth quake' (Ps. 99:1).

J.   "'For all his works are right' -- 'For the sake of thy steadfast love and thy faithfulness' (Ps. 115:1).

K.   "'And his ways are just' -- 'He will judge the peoples with equity' (Ps. 96:10).

L.   "'And those who walk in pride' -- 'The Lord reigns, he is robed in majesty, the Lord is robed, he is girded with strength' (Ps. 93:1).

M.   "'He is able to abase' -- 'All the horns of the wicked he will cut off' (Ps. 75:11)."

N.   "The rock badger" (Lev. 11:5) -- this refers to Media.

O.   "For it chews the cud" -- for it gives praise to the Holy One, blessed be he: "Thus says Cyrus, king of Persia, 'All the kingdoms of the earth has the Lord, the God of the heaven, given me" (Ezra 1:2).

P.   "The hare" -- this refers to Greece.

Q.   "For it chews the cud" -- for it gives praise to the Holy One, blessed be he.

R.   Alexander the Macedonian, when he saw Simeon the Righteous, said, "Blessed be the God of Simeon the Righteous."

S.   "The pig" (Lev. 11:7) -- this refers to Edom.

T.   "For it does not chew the cud" -- for it does not give praise to the Holy One, blessed be he.

U.   And it is not enough that it does not give praise, but it blasphemes and swears violently, saying, "Whom do I have in heaven, and with you I want nothing on earth" (Ps. 73:25).

12. A.   Another interpretation [of GRH, cud, now with reference to GR, stranger:]

B.   "The camel" (Lev. 11:4) -- this refers to Babylonia.

C.   "For it chews the cud" [now: brings up the stranger] -- for it exalts righteous men: "And Daniel was in the gate of the king" (Dan. 2:49).

D.   "The rock badger" (Lev. 11:5) -- this refers to Media.

E.   "For it brings up the stranger" -- for it exalts righteous men: "Mordecai sat at the gate of the king" (Est. 2:19).

F.   "The hare" (Lev. 11:6) -- this refers to Greece.

G.   "For it brings up the stranger" -- for it exalts the righteous.

H.   When Alexander of Macedonia saw Simeon the Righteous, he would rise up on his feet. They said to him, "Can't you see the Jew, that you stand up before this Jew?"

I.   He said to them, "When I go forth to battle, I see something like this man's visage, and I conquer."

J.   "The pig" (Lev. 11:7) -- this refers to Rome.

K. "But it does not bring up the stranger" -- for it does not exalt the righteous.

L. And it is not enough that it does not exalt them, but it kills them.

M. That is in line with the following verse of Scripture: "I was angry with my people, I profaned my heritage; I gave them into your hand, you showed them no mercy; on the aged you made your yoke exceedingly heavy" (Is. 47:6).

N. This refers to R. Aqiba and his colleagues.

13. A. Another interpretation [now treating "bring up the cud" (GR) as "bring along in its train" (GRR)]:

B. "The camel" (Lev. 11:4) -- this refers to Babylonia.

C. "Which brings along in its train" -- for it brought along another kingdom after it.

D. "The rock badger" (Lev. 11:5) -- this refers to Media.

E. "Which brings along in its train" -- for it brought along another kingdom after it.

F. "The hare" (Lev. 11:6) -- this refers to Greece.

G. "Which brings along in its train" -- for it brought along another kingdom after it.

H. "The pig" (Lev. 11:7) -- this refers to Rome.

I. "Which does not bring along in its train" -- for it did not bring along another kingdom after it.

J. And why is it then called "pig" (HZYR)? For it restores (MHZRT) the crown to the one who truly should have it [namely, Israel, whose dominion will begin when the rule of Rome ends].

K. That is in line with the following verse of Scripture: "And saviors will come up on Mount Zion to judge the Mountain of Esau [Rome], and the kingdom will then belong to the Lord" (Ob. 1:21).

To stand back and consider this vast apocalyptic vision of Israel's history, we first review the message of the construction as a whole. This comes in two parts, first, the explicit, then the implicit.

As to the former, the first claim is that God had told the prophets what would happen to Israel at the hands of the pagan kingdoms, Babylonia, Media, Greece, Rome. These are further represented by Nebuchadnezzar, Haman, Alexander for Greece, Edom or Esau, interchangeably, for Rome. The same vision came from Adam, Abraham, Daniel and Moses. The same policy toward Israel -- oppression, destruction, enslavement, alienation from the true God -- emerged from all four.

How does Rome stand out? First, it was made fruitful through the prayer of Isaac in behalf of Esau. Second, Edom is represented by the fourth and final beast. Rome is related through Esau, as Babylonia, Media, and Greece are not. The fourth beast was seen in a vision separate from the first three. It was worst of all and outweighed the rest. In the apocalypticizing of the animals of Lev. 11:4-8/Deut. 14:7, the camel, rock badger, hare, and pig, the pig, standing for Rome, again emerges as different from the others and more threatening than the rest. Just as the pig pretends to be a clean beast by showing the cloven hoof, but in fact is an unclean one, so Rome pretends to be just but in fact governs by thuggery. Edom does not pretend to praise God but only blasphemes. It does not exalt the righteous but kills them. These symbols concede nothing to Christian monotheism and biblicism.

Of greatest importance, while all the other beasts bring further ones in their wake, the pig does not: "It does not bring another kingdom after it." It will restore the crown to the one who will truly deserve it, Israel. Esau will be judged by Zion, so Obadiah 1:21.

Now how has the symbolization delivered an implicit message? It is in the treatment of Rome as distinct, but essentially equivalent to the former kingdoms. This seems to me a stunning way of saying that the now-Christian empire in no way requires differentiation from its pagan predecessors. Nothing has changed, except matters have gotten worse. Beyond Rome, standing in a straight line with the others, lies the true shift in history, the rule of Israel and the cessation of the dominion of the (pagan) nations.

The polemic represented by the symbolization of Christian Rome, therefore, makes the simple point that, first, Christians are no different from, and no better than, pagans; they are essentially the same. Second, just as Israel had survived Babylonia, Media, Greece, so would they endure to see the end of Rome (whether pagan, whether Christian). But of course the symbolic polemic rested on false assumptions, hence conveyed a message that misled Jews by misrepresenting their new enemy. The new Rome really did differ from the old. Christianity was not merely part of a succession of undifferentiated modes of paganism. True, the symbols assigned to Rome attributed worse, more dangerous traits than those assigned to the earlier empires. The pig pretends to be clean, just as the Christians give the signs of adherence to the God of Abraham, Isaac, and Jacob. That much the passage concedes. But it is not enough. For out of symbols should emerge a useful public policy, and the mode of thought represented by symbols in the end should yield an accurate confrontation with that for which the symbol stands.

In fact it would be many centuries before Jews would take seriously, and in its own terms, the claim of Christianity to constitute a kind of Judaism, and not a kind of paganism. It would take a long time for Jews to distinguish the Christian from other outsiders. When that differentiation began to emerge, it would be in Christian Europe, on the part of Joseph Kimhi and Moses Nahmanides and others who had no choice. By that time, to be sure, "paganism" had long disappeared from the world of Israel's residency, on the one hand, and any expectation that Roman rule would give way to Israelite hegemony had lost all worldly credibility. Then, but only then, we find Jews confronting in a systematic way and with solid knowledge of the other side the facts of history that had emerged many centuries earlier.

Whether a different symbolic system would have produced a more realistic and effective policy for the confrontation with triumphant Christianity we shall never know. For so long Israel had pretended nothing happened of any importance, not in the first century, not in the fourth. By the time people came around to concede that, after all, Christianity was here to stay and was essentially different from anything Israel had earlier encountered, it was an awareness too late to make such a difference in Israel's framing of its picture of the outsider and its policy toward the alien.

If we may set into a larger framework the data at hand, we note that Judaism and Christianity in late antiquity present histories that mirror one another. When Christianity began, Judaism was the dominant tradition in the Holy Land and framed its ideas within a political framework until the early fifth century. Christianity there was subordinate and had to work out against the background of a politically definitive Judaism. Elsewhere, of course, Christianity had to work out of its subordinate position as well. From the time of Constantine onward, matters reversed themselves. Now Christianity predominated, expressing its ideas in political and institutional terms. Judaism, by contrast, had lost its political foundations and faced the task of working out its self-understanding in terms of a world defined by Christianity, now everywhere triumphant and in charge of politics. The important shift came in the early fourth century.

In consequence of the original situation, Christians had to attend to the limits of their community, while Jews took for granted they knew their own frontiers. Christians therefore addressed the issue of the outsider and undertook to differentiate one from the next, indeed, as early as Paul's letter to the Romans, taking up the question of Israel "after the flesh." It would be a thousand years before the Jews would find it urgent to take up the question of Israel "after the spirit," the now-ineluctable claim to constitute the heir and successor of the "Old Testament" through the New. To conclude: in future inquiries we wish to ask the framers of the two great traditions to tell us, in a systematic and detailed way, precisely how, in theory at least, they coped with difference within and diversity without. To state matters in the most general way: what theory of "the other" did the great minds of Judaic and Christian antiquity work out, in order to make sense of themselves and outsiders as well? When we know how people defined the other, of course, we grasp how they understood who they themselves were. So we turn back to the beginnings, not to learn merely where we came from. Rather we want to find out how people whom we see as our predecessors worked out problems remarkably congruent to the issues of our own country and age.

In a word, our search for theories of the other encompasses the unfolding consciousness of self, how one group understood itself in the encounter with other groups, how each group made peace, in its own mind, with the presence of many others. When we understand how people made sense of one another and furthermore formulated such sense as they made in terms they could hand on to coming generations and even incorporate in law and institutions, then we will grasp what we seek. The results thus far prove negative. But the consequence is stunning. Nothing that happened appears to have changed Israel's sense of itself. The fact that symbols of the other proved unchanging indicates, I think, that Israel's sense of the self had endured and overcome an awful crisis.

Part Two

SOCIETY AND SYMBOL:
MESSIAH, HISTORY, TORAH AS MODES OF SOCIAL SYMBOLIZATION

Chapter Two

THE CITY AS USELESS SYMBOL IN LATE ANTIQUE JUDAISM

Since in modern and contemporary times the Jews live in very large metropolitan areas, people assume that they have always done so. Consequently, Jews see themselves as an essentially urban group, and metropolitan, cosmopolitan Judaism will take its place among the religions, or ideologies, of mass culture and context. As recently as the nineteenth century, however, the Jews had not yet completed their share in the massive international movement from village to city. That movement was, in fact, a particularly nineteenth and twentieth century phenomenon, a definitive component of modernization and Westernization. When Jews left the villages and towns of Eastern and Central Europe, they quite naturally moved to equivalent social settings, villages and towns of southern and midwestern America, on the one side, and equivalent dorp of the Vaal in South Africa, on the other. The small towns of the South Island in New Zealand have many empty synagogue buildings, and in our own day the Jewish communities close their doors in even medium sized places like Kimberly and Bloomfontein in South Africa. Alabama and Iowa and many New England states contain towns with handsome synagogue buildings but no Jews. The first generation of the uprooted took for granted it would live as it always had, in modest numbers of fully identified Jews in villages that knew who was a Jew and who was not. It was the second, and still more, the third, generation of the uprooted who left for the capital, the metropolis, whether Johannesburg, or Buenos Aires, or Los Angeles, or Tel Aviv.

Whether the world has produced religious traditions distinctively suited to the experience of the city I cannot say. My guess is that the particular context of diversity and anonymity characteristic of city living finds its match, its contrastive complement, in the intensely personal and individual experience of self-selection and conversion characteristic of the newer religions of our own day, whether the rebirth of a kind of Hassidism -- celebration of the Zaddik -- in metropolitan Judaism, or in the flowering of the evangelical churches of twice-born Christians in the great cities of this country, or in the remarkable renewal of Islam in the bazaars of Tehran and Shiraz, or in Jonestown, for that matter. What these communities have in common is the fact that they form intense and vigorous social units, cut off from, yet deeply embedded in, the life of the larger world of diversity and anonymity against which they find definition. All of them focus upon a particular individual, a holy man, a model. To be a Hassid, with distinctive clothing and mannerism and language, moreover, is to be somebody amidst a lot of nobodies. Jonestown, for its part, was born not in Guyana but in San Francisco and Oakland.

Now, more to the point, if we ask what, in the theological or social thought of the distinctively urban and metropolitan communities of our own day, derives from, or responds to, the urban context, we confront a puzzle. On the surface, nothing. There is little explicit reference to context, except to reject its "evils." Yet, underneath, I suspect, a great deal. The theological focus of these communities tends to be anything but social; in creating community, these groups reject the city. In focusing upon the saved individual in radical isolation from the common undifferentiated mass of the damned, the various religions rebuild community where they perceive none. Like the earliest urban Christians, the converts -- whether Jewish to Lubovitch, or Moslem to the Moslem Brotherhood or to the Ayatollah's Iranian version, or Christian to the pentecostal or evangelical churches -- see themselves as going from non-being to being, a social as much as a salvific dimension. The early Christians called themselves a people that is called forth from the peoples, a no-people, a new people.

In all, the urban experience tends, in the world of the soul and the social imagination, not to produce urbanity at all. For what traits of urbane and civil discourse can emerge from people whose inner life speaks of heaven's special grace shining upon them in particular. The acute sense of difference from the unredeemed or unwashed other testifies to the opposite of that conscious, chronic search for sameness and tolerance we think characteristic of large, but not small, places.

Now when we turn to the world of late antiquity -- that is, the first six centuries of the Common Era -- we reach the single most important period in the history of the Jewish people and of Judaism. If we wish to ask about the interplay between cities and the Jews' imaginative life, the social characteristics of the Judaism they created, we therefore had best pay some close attention to the period at hand. For in late antiquity, Judaism as we know it took shape. We speak now of the formative period of Judaism. The social traits of the Jews -- a diverse people, speaking many languages, living in many countries, yet using a single holy language, Hebrew, and facing a single holy place, the Land of Israel and its mother-city, Jerusalem -- then reached final form. Indeed, the promise of the period at hand for the larger inquiry reaches full expression when we speak the word, Jerusalem. For that is not a city, but the city. Even at the outset we realize that what is on the surface an urban locus provided the center and focus for the social imagination of Judaism, then and forever afterward. But the Jews did not live in Jerusalem, and, we shall now see, it was not in cities that they produced Judaism's principal documents after the Hebrew Scriptures, I mean, the Mishnah, Tosefta, Talmud of the Land of Israel, Talmud of Babylonia, Sifra, Sifré on Numbers, Sifré on Deuteronomy, Genesis Rabbah, Leviticus Rabbah, not to mention the Jewish Prayerbook and the translations of the Hebrew Scriptures into Aramaic. Judaism as we know did not come out of cities. All of the books of Judaism in its formative age come to us from towns that you could traverse in not half a morning's walk, and most of them, towns still smaller than that.

Before proceeding to spell out that fact and its consequences, however, let us stand back and ask ourselves two questions, one large, one small: precisely what do we mean by a city? and exactly what in the sources' mind were the building blocks of any social unit, whether village, town, or city? So, I mean to ask, what are the smallest, and what are the largest, components of society, as the ancient Judaic writings by rabbis describe matters.

In the imagination of the framers of the rabbinic writings, the smallest unit of society was the irreducible economic unit, that is, that collectivity that, first, formed in and of itself a whole, working and self-sustaining society, but that, second, could not be further subdivided into other whole and self-sustaining societies. In the rabbinic writings such an irreducible economic unit was headed by the householder, the ba^{c}al habbayit, and, it must follow, the unit itself should be called the house, bayit, or, oikos, yielding in the language we receive from the Greek, the word economy. The irreducible social unit was the irreducible economic unit. Then, in a neat composition of matched building blocks that, in the fantasy of the philosopher-lawyers of the rabbinic writings, constituted society, the village, the town, or the city, will comprise small, medium, and large numbers of economies, households. But reality did not work out that way. My impression is that the village did conform, the city did not conform, and the town only with difficulty conformed, to the rabbinical fantasy of a neat and orderly oecumene -- a construct of households, a composite economy. Let me now amplify the rabbinic conception of society and of the metropolis.

The simple fact is that the smallest whole unit of society for the framers of the Mishnah and their successors in the Tosefta, the two Talmuds, and the compilations of scriptural exegeses known as Midrashim, in no way corresponds to the smallest whole unit of society of the ancient city. For, as I said, the philosophers of the Mishnah perceived the social world to be built out of householders, at the head of which was the effective social unit, the baal habbayit or master of a household. A household consisted of more than the master and his extended family. It constituted an economic unit, including slaves, craftsmen, shepherds and field laborers -- the entire panoply of workers on a farm. Of necessity, moreover, the household encompassed sizable plots of land, some of it sufficiently contiguous to constitute a domain, that is, a private domain, cheek by jowl with other private domains, if also encompassing bits and pieces of land elsewhere. True, the householder was assumed to live in a courtyard, made up of a number of such households, and the courtyard was arranged in an alleyway, made up of a number of such courtyards -- a rather tight hive of people. But the whole then remained essentially pastoral. The town, such as it was, was a place in which farmers, their families and their associated servants, made their lives. And, it must further be said, the town was assumed by the legal texts to be constituted entirely of Jews. Where difference is assumed at the near-at-hand, it is between Israelites of one conviction and those of another: an Israelite who believed in a given rite as against another who denied its efficacy.

When, by contrast, the framers of the Mishnah spoke of a larger social unit than a town, the assumption is that it was not made up entirely or mostly of Jews. Let me give a single graphic illustration of that fact, which also permits us to assess just how much difference that fact made in the larger thought of the philosophers at hand.

When the city as such becomes important in the system of the Mishnah, precisely how does it make its appearance? To answer the question, we take up a concrete case and follow its unfolding. I present it in the language of my student, Howard Schwartz, as he spells out the materials of Mishnah-tractate Uqsin 3:1-3,9. I give only so much of the text and Schwartz's interpretation as we require for our purpose, but enough so that the context and style of discourse become clear. Schwartz translates M. Uqs. 3:3 as follows:

K.   Lo, these [items] are classified as food only if there is an intention (mhsbh) [on the owner's part to use them for human consumption], and [they become susceptible to impurity even] if there is no preparation (i.e., moistening). [The framers cannot determine the status of these things without asking the Israelite his intention].

L.   [The following are examples]: 1) the carcass of a forbidden species of animal [such as a camel] regardless of its location [whether in a village or market place], and 2) an improperly slaughtered bird of a permitted species [such as a pigeon that an Israelite has] in a village.

M.   These [items at L are classified as food only] if there is an intention (mhsbh) [on the owner's part to use them for human consumption], and [they become susceptible to impurity even] if there is no preparation (i.e., moistening). [The Israelite is forbidden to eat these things because they are a forbidden species of animal or because they were slaughtered improperly. Accordingly, the status of these items is uncertain. Will the Israelite throw them away or sell them to a gentile? To resolve the ambiguity, we take account of his intention].

N.   [The following are examples of category IV]: 1) an improperly slaughtered animal of a permitted species [such as a cow], regardless of its location [whether in a village or market place], and 2) an improperly slaughtered bird of a permitted species [such as a pigeon, that an Israelite has] in the market place; and 3) the fat [from an animal of a forbidden species that an Israelite is carrying] in the market place.

O.   Lo, these [items at N. may become susceptible to uncleanness even] if there is no preparation (i.e., moistening), and [they are classified as food even] if there is no intention (mhsbh) [on the owner's part to use them for human consumption. The expectation is that he will sell them to a gentile because in one case he is in the market place (2) and in the other case the animal is extremely valuable (1). They are classified as food, therefore, regardless of what the owner intends].

What is important for our inquiry is the fact that the Mishnah's framers take account, in particular, of whether food is located in a village or in a city. Schwartz explains as follows:

When the framers of this Mishnah can classify a foodstuff according to its normal use, they ignore the owner's plan. In the following rules, the framers consider food substances whose status they cannot determine on the basis of Israelite norms. This difficulty arises because Israelites put certain types of things to more than one use. Even in resolving this ambiguity, the framers appeal to subjective criteria only as a last resort. First, they invoke three objective criteria: 1) the location of the foodstuff (whether in a town's market place or a village), 2) its value (can the Israelite afford to discard it?) and, 3) its marketability (will gentiles buy it?).

Schwartz's comment pertinent to our inquiry is an follows:

> The framers consider the object's location. If they see an Israelite carrying a fish of a forbidden species in the town market place, Mishnah's philosophers classify it as food. Why? Since the Israelite stands not in the village [which is all Jewish] but the market place [of a town, where there also are gentiles], they assume he will sell this fish rather than throw it away. When the Israelite carries the same fish in his village, however, we can no longer be sure what he will do. On the one hand, he may decide to throw it away, [since he has no gentile near at hand]. On the other hand, he may choose to look for a gentile buyer [who may happen by]. Therefore, to determine what he will do, the framers must ask him his plan.

From what Schwartz says, two assumptions of the law become clear. First of all, the framers take for granted that the inhabitants of a village will be mainly Jews. Second, they assume that some of the inhabitants of a town large enough to support a market will not be Jews. It follows that a trait of a town, all the more so of a city will be different from a trait of a village; the former will be made up of Jews, the latter will be large, mixed, and diverse.

I have dwelt on this matter at some length to show that the passage at hand contains assumptions about the character of Israelite settlement, on the one side, and of cities and villages, on the other. These assumptions seem to me to enjoy the status of facts, simply because people may be assumed to know what they are talking about when the facts do not serve a controverted or polemical purpose and in no way contradict what we know from other evidence. The assumption that we must distinguish, as to the Jews' condition, between settlements that were small and wholly Jewish and those that were large and mixed bears several important implications for the problem at hand -- how Jews thought about, or experienced, large-scale metropolitan life in late antiquity. But before we proceed, let me spell out some well known facts that, in general, exemplify the suppositions on the Jews semi-rural condition revealed in the Mishnah-passage Schwartz has laid out for us.

Overall, in both the Land of Israel and Babylonia, Jews lived in three types of settlements, large metropolitan ones, in which they cannot have formed a significant part of the total population; towns, in which they probably formed a sizable minority; and villages "of their own," by which I mean, settlements constituted principally by Jews. In the Land of Israel, Caesarea represents the first category, Tiberias the second, possibly also Sepphoris and Lud, and the numerous villages, only a few of them actually named, to which allusion is made casually or not all, the third. In Babylonia the great metropolis was Seleucia-Ctesiphon, on the banks of the Tigris, into which the Royal Canal flowed from the Euphrates. The former was Greek, the latter Iranian. Jews lived in nearby Nehardea. There were towns represented as having large Jewish populations but not as consisting mainly of Jews, such as Dura-Europos in Mesopotamia, and Nehardea in Babylonia, and then there were Jewish villages, such as the nameless one on the Royal Canal destroyed by the Emperor Julian in his invasion in A.D. 360. We have no idea what proportions of the entire Jewish population lived in places of the three classifications. My general impression is that most people lived in villages and worked on farms, a few as householders, a great many as landless workers or sharecroppers. But that impression derives from texts which, as I said to begin with, represent Israel as a composite of householders, landowners and their dependents, employees and slaves. These law codes portray the principal points of legislative concern essentially as householders will have defined them. The corpus of rabbinic literature speaks about a farming people, not a trading one. Among the farmers were craftsmen, on the one side, and an enormous class of very poor workers, on the other. What have all these folk to do with a city? The answer is, very little. The entire urban experience of late antiquity lies beyond the world of the ancient Jews, as that world is represented by the rabbinic literature.

So much for the sages' imagination of the household, town, and city. The difference between town and city was trivial. It consisted of the fact that, while in a town, pretty much everyone was Jewish, in a city, there were gentiles -- an undifferentiated mass of faceless people, all of them falling into the same classification of "non-Jews." But what were cities really like? The first trait, in contrast to the rabbis' fantasy of neat blocks, was their diversity. For rabbis "non-Jew" was a category that encompassed nearly the whole world. But it hardly sufficed to classify the rest. More important, so far as the rabbis imagined any urban unit, from village on upward, to be made up of social-economic units, "households," or whole "economies," they were wrong on that count too. For the city was not a neat construction of matching blocks, that is, economic units. The urban society's components were of diverse types. They fell into a range of entirely distinct categories. The building blocks of a city's population did not comprise diverse species of a single genus, "economic unit." They revealed more than one genus, so proved incomparable to one another. Their diversity constituted the sole universally applicable definition for the social units of which a city was made up. And that fact, by itself, is trivial. To follow up on this matter, we turn to the results of the most recent study of religion in the ancient city, Wayne A. Meeks, The First Urban Christians. The Social World of the Apostle Paul (New Haven, 1983: Yale University Press).

In describing the apostle, Paul, Meeks begins his account: "Paul was a city person. The city breathes through his language. Jesus' parables of sowers and weeds, share-croppers and mud-roofed cottages call forth smells of manure and earth, and the Aramaic of the Palestinian villages often echoes in the Greek. [Paul] seems more at home with the cliches of Greek rhetoric, drawn from gymnasium, stadium, or workshop. Moreover, Paul was among those who depended on the city for their livelihood." Now the contrast between the one and the other -- Jesus, or the Mishnah's rabbis, as townsfolk and village people, Paul as a man of the city and the metropolis -- should bear consequences. Specifically, we ought to be able to point, in the thought and the system of the city-bred thinker, to traits of mind, modes of thought, perhaps even specific propositions, that respond to or emerge from the urban condition. We should be able to discern, along these same lines, where and how the consequences of living in a corporate society of people of one mind and heart have helped to shape the perspectives of the villagers or townsfolk about whom the Mishnah speaks. I cannot think of a more vivid challenge to our capacity to imagine and reflect and speculate. Yet, to this time, I also cannot point to any systematic but also credible picture of why the great city led people to think in one way and reach one sort of conclusion, while the small town led other people to think in some other way and reach another sort of conclusion. There are such works that relate the sociology to the theology of a given tractate, e.g., the great work by John Elliott, Home to the Homeless, on First Peter. But these are rare to begin with, and controverted in scholarly debate even now.

Yet we do know things about the great cities of antiquity, and we can draw some conclusions from their character as social entities. We already have noticed that, to the framers of the Mishnah, the great city and marketplace presented diversity: gentiles of various kinds (among whom rabbis were reluctant to differentiate), idolatry and danger; but also vitality and enormous busy-ness. In fact, cities formed the spearhead of the processes of change that, from the time of Alexander onward, would continue to shake the foundations of the traditional Middle East. The countryfolk spoke diverse languages -- "place-talk," we would say in Pidgin -- while the cities spoke the international language, Greek in the east, Latin in the West. The countryside lived by the natural calendar, citing the sacred calendar in relationship to the movement of the moon and the seasons of the sun. The city superimposed yet another calendar, one framed of politics, the birthday of the king, for example. The countryside was diffuse and its cultures cogent and individual. The city was the center of the world. Meeks quotes Rostovtzeff: "The Roman Empire was to become a commonwealth of self-governing cities." The cities housed the courts of law and administration. Influence flowed from the standard of firm government, Roman government, rather than from the charisma of the local big man. In the towns people recognized the big man and responded to his wish and will. In the cities they fantasized not about a particular individual, whom people recognized and knew, but about a holy man as a general type or category: faceless mediator, everywhere the same.

But in the cities people clung to difference. Meeks says, "Noncitizen residents often retained some sense of ethnic identity by establishing local cults of their native gods or by forming a voluntary association, which also had at least the trappings of religion..." Now what difference did these distinctions actually make? How did the city relate to the country? True, the city depended upon its suburbs and the towns upon the city. But, as Ramsay MacMullen describes matters (cited by Meeks, p. 14):

> Economic ties between urban and rural centers are thus of the closest. They are not [however] friendly. The two worlds regard each other as, on the one side, clumsy, brutish, ignorant, uncivilized; on the other side, as baffling, exortionate, arrogant. Peasants who move to a town feel overwhelmed by its manners and dangers and seek out relatives or previous emigrants from the same village...

So, Meeks concludes, "The cities were where power was," and, he says, "The conservatism of the villages preserved their diversity; changes in the city were in the direction of a common Greco-Roman culture." In the city people moved, sometimes even upward. In the country, they stayed put. Women, for example, married upward or downward, crossed boundaries that in the towns they would hardly approach. Tradition, in context, meant stability, confinement.

Any account of the ancient city will tell us, also, that Jews lived in cities. But, as I said, for the Land of Israel and for Babylonia, the Jews were not a city people. And those two countries produced the documents of Judaism that have predominated from their day to ours. The urbane philosopher, Philo, son of the Jewry of one of the world's great cities,

Alexandria in Egypt, Paul, whom Meeks presents as a first urban Christian, a Jew from Tarsus who went from city to city -- these figures out of ancient Judaism disappeared from the world of Judaism. But the writings of the villages and the towns, of Tiberias and Sepphoris, Pumbedita and Nehardea -- those endured and laid out the boundaries for the Judaism of the future. My best guess is that this same form of Judaism persisted for as long as it did because, in large measure, the social and historical conditions that defined its initial message and dictated its relevance persisted for long afterward. The corporate community of Israel living essentially by itself endured until the processes of urbanization imposed upon the Jewish people social conditions lacking all precedent. Then the Judaism of the town and village also faced competition from new, more urban and differentiating, kinds. But this is now a mere guess.

We therefore ask not about a single passage of a rabbinical writing, such as the one set forth so ably by Howard Schwartz, but about whole documents. Instead of a close reading of one text, we insert a probe through two very large ones. Specifically, we review references to the city in two quite different documents, the Mishnah, the first legal text of Judaism after the Mosaic law codes, ca. A.D. 200, and Leviticus Rabbah, one of the earliest compositions of materials organized around the framework of Scripture, specifically, the book of Leviticus, ca. A.D. 400.

When we omit references to a city or town in which the urban context plays no differentiating role, what do we find in the Mishnah's repertoire? I discern remarkably few allusions to an urban setting in which that setting makes much difference. For example, when people refer to a city on which it has not rained (M. Ta. 2:1), or a city that has been taken in a siege (M. Ket. 2:9), there is no consequence I can see for a larger theory of the difference between a village or town and a city. On the other hand, when, at M. Qid. 2:3, we find a clear reference to the difference between life in the one place and that in the other, we do reach a point of some interest. The passage has a man falsely swear to a prospective bride that he is a villager when, in fact, he lives in the city, or vice versa. The unmet stipulation nullifies the woman's agreement to become betrothed to him. A husband may not take his wife from a town to a city and vice versa, M. Ketubot 13:10D. So there was a clear difference. But why the difference matters is not specified. Nor does the equivalent distinction make a difference at M. Megillah 2:3. I find no tendency to evaluate life in the one sort of place as better, or as worse, than life in the other; the location is simply a fact of life. The notion of dwelling together with gentiles in the same city is a commonplace, e.g., M. Makhshirin 2:5. Likewise, there are references to large and small cities, e.g., M. Erubin 5:8, and these references produce no grounds to think sages held a higher opinion of one than of the other. A large city is defined as one in which there are ten men of leisure, so M. Megillah 1:3, and a small town, one in which there are fewer than that number. The usage of KPR, small town, is unusual; generally the framers of the Mishnah use the word for town, ^{C}YR, sometimes clearly meaning a large one, sometimes a small one, and often with no clear intent. That, sum and substance, is the whole story for the Mishnah. There is a clear and present distinction between city and town. But it makes very little difference. Where it does make a difference I cannot say what that difference is.

For the second part of the present inquiry I turn to Leviticus Rabbah, a rather coherent composition on themes present in the book of Leviticus. The composition is generally believed to have reached closure in the late fourth or early fifth century, so we may use as our convenience-date the year 400. It derives from the Land of Israel. It portrays things as they were perceived by rabbis, probably flourishing over the preceding century or less. At that time the Jews of the Land of Israel lived under the now-Christian empire of Rome centered in Byzantium, a great city and an empire of great cities. The Jews were part of an unimportant hinterland; they lived mainly in Galilee, while the chief city of the place, Caesarea, was on the coast. The Jews moreover communicated through such coastal towns as Kezib and the Ladder of Tyre and Acco and Sidon, but, in the main, inhabited farming villages round about. The area was of mixed population. Mainly Jewish settlements were scattered among other settlements; areas were known to be "gentile" or "Samaritan" or otherwise distinctive to a given group. But taken together, if each group were given a color to mark its settlements, then the map of the area would be speckled in many colors, exhibiting few broad stripes or large spots indicative of the dominance of some one group. That is the background. What in fact does the document at hand have to tell us about the city, whether in general or Caesarea in particular, or Sidon or Tyre or Tiberias or Sepphoris or Kezib or Lud (in the south). I survey my translation of Margulies' superb text (Mordecai Margulies, Midrash Wayyikra Rabbah. A critical edition based on manuscripts and Genizah fragments with variants and notes [Jerusalem, 1953-1960] 1-5). To give some idea of the dimensions of the text: Margulies' text runs 868 pages in Hebrew type, each page containing from four to ten lines of text; my translation runs more than 900 pages in typescript. So we are dealing with a rather sizable document. Let me now list all the pertinent passages:

I:VIII.2:   A king makes a tour of a province, bringing with him various officers.

IV:II.3:   A townsman who married a princess can never fully carry out his obligations to treat her in a special way.

VI:II.1:   The governor of Caesarea would merely flog the thieves, but he would execute the fences.

XXII:IV.5:   A messenger was carrying evil decrees against the Jews of Caesarea.

XXX:VII.1:   There is the case of a town which owed arrears to the king, who went to collect what was owed him, but remitted the tax when he was greeted properly.

Self-evidently, our probe produces little of substance. In the case of Leviticus Rabbah, references to "the city" as an abstraction, as an organizing category, or as a symbol simply are not to be found. In the case of the Mishnah, there is a clear distinction between village or town and city; they constitute separate categories. But, as I said, we do not know what difference the distinction actually makes. It constitutes merely a line one may not cross, e.g., when one categorizes himself in relationship to a prospective bride. I detect no preference for village over town or city, simply the recognition that life for the woman in the one is different from what it is in the other. So what!

It remains to ask, What of Jerusalem? It was, after all, supposed to be the city, the metropolis, of Judaism. One may wonder why I have not turned attention to either visions of Jerusalem as a city or projections upon the Jerusalem in heaven of then-contemporary experience. Jews inherited in Scripture a sizable corpus of images and myths associated with the heavenly city, poised as it was in heaven over the earthly Jerusalem. Certainly all Israel hoped for the rebuilding of Jerusalem and the reestablishment of the Temple. The law itself made ample provision for life in Jerusalem. Whole tractates, such as Maaser Sheni, took up the definition of the city and of food that has entered the sacred limits of the city. Others, such as Sheqalim, dealt with the officials of the city and the Temple and their work. And yet, if we wish to know about how Jews in late antiquity entered into city life, defined its issues, accomodated to its challenges -- to all this "Jerusalem" bears no relationship whatsoever. To Israel Jerusalem on earth from 135 was a dead city; they could go there only to mourn, and then on only a few days a year. Jerusalem in heaven was precisely that; a heavenly city, with its own character and composition. The heavenly city in no way related to earthly realities, neither drawing on nor supplying metaphors for this world's city.

So far as I can see, when Jews spoke of Jerusalem in heaven, or of Jerusalem in time to come, they did not project fantasies about a better life in a city imagined as the equivalent to or the opposite of the cities they then knew. My guess is that there is a simple reason. The city as such lay beyond the social experience of the rabbis who produced and preserved our literary sources. They entered no encounter with the city, either as an abstraction, or as something concrete and ominous in their lives. Living elsewhere than in a metropolis, they had no notion of how to construct, in their minds, something better than, something opposite to, the metropolis they would have known and rejected. So when they spoke of Jerusalem, it was not with the intention of describing a better city than village in which they lived. Jerusalem stood for something else, sui generis, something with no analogy down here in the village or town -- or city. The reason, as I have said, is that the metropolis in heaven in now way was meant to compare to, to contrast with, the known village on earth.

To sum up: a town constituted an economic unit, composed of economic units: a group of households, made up of individual households, a household being the irreducible economic unit of the society known to (or imagined by) sages. To such a neat and orderly world, cities defied all powers of rabbis' imagination. Their diversity, their chaos, their opportunity, their provision of roles for the unlike, the woman, the slave, the foreigner -- these traits of society in the urban setting lay wholly outside of the experience of society reflected in the rabbinic literature.

To conclude, we must emphasize that, for the rabbis of late antiquity, cities formed part of the larger issue of the outside world, the gentile realm. True, enormous Jewish populations dwelled in Alexandria, both Syrian Antiochs, Sardis, Rome, Dura-Europos (probably also Seleucia-Ctesiphon). But most rabbis did not come from such places and, so far as we know, none conducted his master-disciple-circles in them. (The sole exception is Caesarea in Abbahu's day.) The documents that portray Judaism -- and these are the sole literary evidence out of late antiquity -- come from villages and towns, not cities.

We have to ask ourselves whether that fact makes a difference for what is in those documents: does the Judaism that took shape in late antiquity speak not only out, but also for and in behalf, of a distinctive viewpoint on the world, shaped in the social ecology of the village, the backward Aramaic-speaking hinterland?

Let us begin with an affirmative observation. The Judaism that reaches full expression in the documents of late antique rabbinical circles addresses a world in which Israel, the Jewish people, lives an essentially autonomous life. To be sure, whether in the Land of Israel or in Babylonia, the Jews recognize the existence of both gentiles in general and gentile governments in particular. But gentiles exist as an outer backdrop, and the governments -- Iranian, Christian-Roman -- as powerful forces to be placated and kept at a distance. The chronic issues of life, the acute crises -- these arose from the inner world of autonomous Israel. At the heart and soul of the ancient system stood the issue of sanctification, of how Israel, having lost the Temple from which holiness had flowed, might yet attain that condition of sanctification that defined its being. At the end and purpose of the system lay the end of time, the coming of the messiah, when, through God's final act of sanctification, hence of the perfection of creation, the world would reenter that condition that it had enjoyed, for a moment, at the outset of sanctification and perfection, in the completion of creation. What did all of this have to do with that urban world, viewed from afar and kept at a distance? Very little.

Now it would constitute an act of gross oversimplification to declare that that view of a corporate Israel above historical time and riding out the waves of history emerged out of definition in the social reality of a nation living isolated in its own villages and towns. But it is correct to observe that the social datum -- the given of the world as viewed by the rabbinic thinkers -- indeed did correspond in a remarkably accurate way to the fundamental traits of the social world in which Israel lived out its life. For Israel in the Land of Israel and in Babylonia, as I have stressed, did see a world made up mostly of itself at the near at hand, of the other and the outsider far away. Jews were of infinitely various sorts, sharply and subtly differentiated. Gentiles were pretty much all alike. Idolatry was idolatry; little effort went into distinguishing one cult from another. The advent even of the Christian empire made remarkably little difference to the framers of the Talmud of the Land of Israel, who never found it necessary to distinguish Christianity from paganism, on the one side, or Christian Rome from pagan Rome, on the other. Esau remained Esau, Edom remained Edom, whoever ruled. Not to know that people revering the same ancient Scriptures that Israel held sacred now ruled in Rome, not to acknowledge that paganism in its gross form had given way to a religion speaking about Israel and claiming to constitute a piece of Israel -- that seems to me a deliberate act of self-delusion, and it is precisely what the later third and fourth century rabbis did in the pages of the Talmud of the Land of Israel.

I cannot imagine that the Talmud of the Land of Israel could have taken that delusive position, were it produced in one of the cosmopolitan centers, such as Alexandria, Antioch, or Byzantium itself. True, a piece of it -- Baba Qamma, Baba Mesia, and Baba Batra -- is alleged to have come to closure in Caesarea in ca. A.D. 350. But that piece contains so little material of an other-than-legal character that we can scarcely judge what, if anything, the rabbis of Caesarea saw or included to reflect the larger world that they confronted from day to day. Because the rabbis of the two Talmuds and of the collections of exegesis of Scripture lived, in the main, mostly among other Jews, in towns that formed corporate Jewish communities, they saw things one way and not some other. Their consciousness of the world within permitted them to perceive the other, the outsider, as part of an undifferentiated world without, a world that scarcely mattered. Such a view of the other, the outsider, proved congruent only to a social experience in which the outsider scarcely made an appearance as a differentiated human being, and in which the things that made outsiders different from one another made no powerful impact upon Israelite (or rabbinical) consciousness.

That is to say, in a diverse world, diversity proves consequential. In an essentially uniform community, it does not. The Talmuds come to us mainly from people who lived chiefly within circles of other Jews. Their vision of the world derives from an experience of social coherence, isolation from difference, indifference to diversity. The Talmuds concentrate on the inner world of Israel, seeing one Jew as a sinner, another as a saint, speaking a language in which "Israel" stood not for a small and isolated minority, but the heart and soul and center of diverse society. If, therefore, I had to point to a single consequence of the essentially small-town setting in which Judaism as we know it took shape, it is the simple fact that, in its formative centuries, Judaism saw Israel, the Jewish people, as landed, settled, and normal people, exhibiting no acute sense of self-con- sciousness and difference of a cultural or ethnic character. Judaism saw Israel as deeply differentiated, hence normal, close to hand, subject to near-sighted analysis, specifically because in its social world, that is pretty much how things were. My best guess is that when the Jews found themselves in a world in which their small numbers in great cities rendered them distinguished and special, acutely different, then the Judaism of corporate and coherent society had to make provision for a new sort of social experience. That experience was one of intense self-consciousness, one in which the Jews were Jews before they were differentiated persons, and in which the presence and power of the gentile world imposed upon the Jews that acute self-awareness of being "Israel" that, in ancient times, we find in the rabbinical writings only when the writers meditate on enormous historical and national issues.

Chapter Three

MISHNAH AND MESSIAH

i.   The Mishnah in the Context of Earlier Uses of the Messiah Theme

When the Temple of Jerusalem fell to the Babylonians in 586 B.C., Israelite thinkers turned to the writing of history to explain what had happened. From that time onward, with the composition of the Pentateuch and the historical books, Joshua, Judges, Samuel, and Kings, to teach the lessons of history, and of prophetic and apocalyptic books to interpret and project those lessons into the future, Israel explained the purpose of its being by focusing upon the meaning of events. The critical issue then was salvation: from what? for what? by whom? In that context, the belief in a supernatural man, an anointed savior or Messiah, formed a natural complement to a system in which teleology took the form of eschatology. Israelites do their duty because of what is happening and of where events will lead. All things point to a foreordained end, presenting the task of inter- preting the signs of the times. No wonder, then, that, when the Temple of Jerusalem fell to the Romans, in A.D. 70, established patterns of thinking guided writers of Judaic apocalypse to pay attention to the meaning of history. In that setting, Jesus, whom Paul had earlier grasped in an essentially ahistoric framework, now turned out, in the hands of the writers of the Gospels, to be Israel's Messiah. He was the Messiah at the end of time, savior and redeemer of Israel from its historical calamity, thus a historical-political figure: king of the Jews.

The character of the Israelite Scriptures, with the emphasis upon historical narrative as a mode of theological explanation, leads us to expect Judaism to evolve as a deeply Messianic religion. With all prescribed actions pointed toward the coming of the Messiah at the end of time, and all interest focused upon answering the historical-salvific questions, "how long?" Judaism from late antiquity to the present day presents no surprises. Its liturgy evokes historical events to prefigure salvation; prayers of petition repeatedly turn to the speedy coming of the Messiah; and the experience of worship invariably leaves the devotee expectant and hopeful. Just as Rabbinic (now-normative) Judaism is a deeply Messianic religion, secular extensions of Judaism for their part have commonly proposed secularized versions of the established pattern of focus upon history and interest in the purpose and denouement of events. Teleology once more takes the form of eschatology embodied in messianic symbols.

Yet, for a brief moment, a vast and influential document presented a kind of Judaism in which history did not define the main framework, in which the issue of teleology took a form other than the familiar, eschatological one, and, in consequence, in which historical events were absorbed, through their trivialization in taxonomic structures, into a non-historical system. In the kind of Judaism at hand in this document, messiahs did figure. But these "anointed men" played no historical role. They undertook a task quite different from that assigned to Jesus by the framers of the Gospels. Messiahs were merely a species of priest, falling into one classification rather than another.

That document is the Mishnah, ca. A.D. 200, a strange corpus of normative statements we may, though with some difficulty, classify as a law code or a school book for philosophical jurists. The difficulty of classification derives from the contents of the document, which deal with the topics to the bulk of which we should be reluctant to assign the title, law. Composed in an age in which, on the Roman side as well, people were making law codes, the Mishnah presents a systematic account of the life of Israel, the Jewish people in the Land of Israel. The Mishnah comprises sixty-three tractates covering six categories of activity. These begin, first, with rules for the conduct of the economy, that is, agriculture, with special attention to the farmers' provision of priestly rations. Second come rules for various special holy days and seasons, with special attention to the conduct of the sacrifical service and life of the Temple cult on such occasions, and corresponding conduct in the home. Third are rules governing the status of women, with particular interest in the transfer of a woman from the domain of one man to that of another. Fourth is a code of civil laws, covering all aspects of commercial, civil, and criminal law, and offering a blueprint for an Israelite government based on the Temple in Jerusalem and headed by a king and a high priest. Fifth, we find rules for the Temple's sacrificial service and for the upkeep of the Temple buildings and establishment, with emphasis upon the life of the cult on ordinary days. Finally, the Mishnah details taboos affecting the cultic life in the form of unclean things and rules on how to remove their effects.

This brief account of the document points toward its principal point of interest: sanctification. At issue is the life of Israel under the aspect of holiness, lived out in relationship to the Temple and under the governance of the priesthood. What has been said indicates also what the document neglects to treat: salvation, that is, the historical life of the Jewish nation, and where it is heading and how to get there. The Mishnah omits all reference to its own point of origin, thus lacking a historical account or a mythic base. The framers of the code likewise barely refer to Scripture, rarely produce proof texts for their own propositions, never imitate the modes of speech of ancient Hebrew, as do the writers of the Dead Sea Scrolls at Qumran. They hardly propose to explain the relationship between their book and the established holy Scriptures of Israel. As we shall see, the absence of sustained attention to events and a doctrine of history serves also to explain why the Messiah as an eschatological figure makes no appearance in the system of the Mishnah.

Accordingly, the later decades of the second century, after the defeat of Bar Kokhba, witnessed the composition of the Mishnah, a vast book, later received as authoritative and turned into the foundations of the two Talmuds, one composed in Babylonia, the other in the Land of Israel, which define Judaism as we know it. If, then, we ask about the context in which this foundation-document of the rabbinic canon came into being, we find ourselves in an age that had witnessed yet another messianic war, fought by Israel against Rome, this under Bar Kokhba, from 132 to 135. That war, coming three generations after the destruction of the Temple, aimed to regain Jerusalem and rebuild the Temple. It seems probable that Bar Kokhba in his own day was perceived as a messianic general, and the war as coming at the expected end of time, the eschatological climax to the drama begun in 70. If so, the character of the Mishnah, the work of the survivors of the war, proves truly astonishing. Here, as I said, we have an immense, systematic and encompassing picture of the life of Israel, in which events scarcely play a role. History never intervenes. The goal and purpose of it all find full and ample expression with scarcely a word about either the end of time or the coming of Messiah. In a word, the Mishnah presents us with a kind of Judaism possessed of an eschatology -- a theory of the end -- without Messiah, a teleology beyond time. When the point of insistence is sanctification, not salvation, in the Mishnah, we see the outcome.

ii.   The Messiah in the Mishnah

We now ask the Mishnah to answer the questions at hand. What of the Messiah? When will he come? To whom, in Israel, will he come? And what must, or can, we do, while we wait, to hasten his coming? If we now reframe these questions divested of their mythic cloak, we ask about the Mishnah's theory of the history and destiny of Israel and the purpose of the Mishnah's own system in relationship to Israel's present and end: the implicit teleology of the philosophical law at hand.

Answering these questions out of the resources of the Mishnah is not possible. The Mishnah presents no large view of history. It contains no reflection whatever on the nature and meaning of the destruction of the Temple in A.D. 70, an event which surfaces only in connection with some changes in the law explained as resulting from the end of the cult. The Mishnah pays no attention to the matter of the end-time. The word "salvation" is rare, "sanctification," in numerous forms, is commonplace. More strikingly, virtually silent on the teleology of its own system, the framers of the Mishnah never tell us why we should do what the Mishnah tells us, let alone explain what will happen if we do. Incidents in the Mishnah are preserved either as narrative settings for the statement of the law, or, occasionally, as precedents. Historical events are classified and turned into entries on lists. But incidents in any case come few and far between. True, events do make an impact. But it always is for the Mishnah's own purpose and within its own taxonomic system and list-making, rule-seeking mode of thought. To be sure, the framers of the Mishnah may also have had a theory of the Messiah and of the meaning of Israel's history and destiny. But they kept it hidden, and their document manages to provide an immense account of Israel's life without explicitly telling us about such matters. To what may be implicit I confess myself blind and deaf: I see and hear only thin echoes of a timeless eternity governed by orderly rules.

Let me digress to provide an important qualification to the argument that is to come. Since the Mishnah constitutes the foundation-document of its kind of Judaism, our interest is in that document as such, and not in other ideas that may or may not also have been held by its framers. Of these the Mishnah tells us nothing. What is assigned or attributed to them in later documents testifies only to what the framers of those documents thought their predecessors had stated long ago. Whether or not the Mishnah's authorities had actually made such statements we do not know. In the Mishnah we have ample evidence concerning the statements they did make in the document for which, along with Scripture, they secured recognition as Israel's constitution. Accordingly, the Mishnah, and the Mishnah alone, defines the original boundaries of the canon of Judaism as the rabbinic system. Whatever else second century thinkers may have believed surfaced only later on. It was not until the third or fourth or fifth centuries that these other opinions, allegedly held in the second century, proved important and made their impact upon the public and collective statement in literature coming forth from rabbinical institutions and defining rabbinic Judaism. So in the Mishnah we deal with what was official and definitive at the beginnings.

Now, to return to the argument, when we walk the frontiers laid out by the Mishnah, we turn inward to gaze upon a portrait of the world at rest, in which, as I said, events take place, but history does not. It is a world of things in the right place, each with its proper name, all in the appropriate classification. In the Mishnah's world, all things aim at stasis both in nature and in society, with emphasis upon proper order and correct form. As we saw, the world of the Mishnah in large part encompasses the cult, the priesthood, and protection of the cult from sources of danger and uncleanness. So the Mishnah presents a priestly conception of the world, creating a system aimed at the sanctification of Israel under the rule of the priests, as a holy people. The world subject to discussion encompasses a Temple, whose rules are carefully studied; a high priest, whose actions are meticulously chronicled; a realm of the clean and the holy, whose taboos are spelled out in exquisite detail.

But, since none of these things existed when the framers of the Mishnah wrote about them, the Mishnah turns out to be something other than what it appears. It purports to describe how things are. But it tells us about a fantasy much more than about the real, palpable world, the world concretely known to the people who wrote about it. So the Mishnah is a work of imagination -- using bits and pieces of facts, to be sure -- made up in the minds of the framers of the Mishnah. The Mishnah does not undertake a description of a real building out there, maintained by real flesh-and-blood people, burning up kidneys of real lambs whose smoke you can smell and see. It is all a realm of made-up memories, artificial dreams, hopes, yearnings. When we turn from the inner perspective to the sheltering world beyond, we see how totally fantastic was the fantasy. For the Mishnah provides prescriptions for preserving a world of stable order. But, living in the aftermath of Bar Kokhba's defeat, the framers of the Mishnah in fact carried on through chaos and crisis, paying the psychic, as much as the political, costs of catastrophic defeat.

Lacking a Temple or credible hope for one, for the first time in Israelite history in the millenium from the rule of David onward, the sages confronted an Israel without blood-rites to atone for sin and win God's favor. Under the circumstances, their minds might well have turned back to the time of David, therefore forward to the age in which David's heir and successor would come to restore the Temple and to rule Israel as God's anointed. Perhaps they did. Maybe in writing the Mishnah, they meant to describe how David's son would do things just as David had done things long ago. But if that was their purpose, they did not say so. And the one thing any student of the Mishnah knows is that

its framers are pitiless in giving detail, in saying everything they wish, and in holding back
-- so far as we can tell -- nothing we might need to know to plumb their meaning.

Yet we do not have to argue from their silence to find out what was in their minds.
True, they speak little of the Messiah and rarely refer to events perceived as history. But
they do record the events of the day when it serves their purposes. They do hint at the
Messiah's coming. So, rather than harping on the absence of evidence, let us rapidly
survey some facts. If, for example, they give us no doctrine of the Messiah, no stories
about him, no account of where he will come from, how we shall know him, and what he
will do, still, they do use the word, "messiah." How do they use it?

In a legal context, the Mishnah's framers know the anointing of a leader, in
connection with two officials: the high priest consecrated with oil, in contrast to the one
consecrated merely by receiving the additional garments that indicate the office of high
priest (M. Mak. 2:6, M. Meg. 1:9, M. Hor. 3:4), and the (high) priest anointed for the
purpose of leading the army in war (M. Sot. 7:2, 8:1, M. Mak. 2:6). When the Mishnah uses
the word messiah, in legal contexts the assumed meaning is always the anointed priest (M.
Hor. 2:2, 3, 7, 3:4, 5).

Yet the Mishnah's framers know a quite separate referent for the same term. When
they wish to distinguish between this age and the world to come, they speak (M. Ber. 1:5)
of "this world and the days of the Messiah." That Messiah can only be the anointed savior
of Israel. The reference is casual, the language routine, the purpose merely factual.
Likewise, at M. Sot. 9:9-15 there is a reference to "the footsteps of the Messiah," again in
the setting of the end of time and the age to come. That passage, a systematic
eschatology, is critical for us in assessing whatever the Mishnah offers as a theory of
Israel's history, so we shall review it in its entirety. (Biblical verses are cited in italics.)

M. Sotah 9:9-15

9:9

I.   A.   When murderers become many, the rite of breaking the heifer's neck was
                cancelled.

        B.   [This was] when Eleazar b. Dinai came along, and he was also called Tehinah b.
                Perishah. Then they went and called him, "Son of a murderer."

II.   C.   When adulterers became many, the ordeal of the bitter water was cancelled.

        D.   And Rabban Yohanan b. Zakkai cancelled it, since it is said, _I will not punish_
                your daughters when they commit whoredom, nor your daughters-in-law when
                they commit adultery, for they themselves go apart with whores (Hos. 4:14).

III.   E.   When Yose b. Yoezer of Seredah and Yose b. Yohanan of Jerusalem died, the
                grape-clusters were cancelled,

        F.   since it is said, _There is no cluster to eat, my soul desires the first ripe fig_
                (Mic. 7:1).

9:10

        A.   Yohanan, high priest, did away with the confession concerning tithe.

        B.   Also: He cancelled the rite of the Awakeners and the Stunners.

        C.   Until his time a hammer did strike in Jerusalem.

        D.   And in his time no man had to ask concerning doubtfully tithed produce.

9:11

IV.   A.   When the Sanhedrin was cancelled, singing at wedding feasts was cancelled, since it is said, <u>They shall not drink wine with a song</u> (Is. 24:9).

9:12

V.   A.   When the former prophets died out, the Urim and Tummim were cancelled.

VI.   B.   When the sanctuary was destroyed, the Shamir-worm ceased and [so did] the honey of <u>supim</u>.

       C.   And faithful men came to an end,

       D.   since it is written, <u>Help, O Lord, for the godly man ceases</u> (Ps. 12:2).

       E.   Rabban Simeon b. Gamaliel says in the name of R. Joshua, "From the day on which the Temple was destroyed, there is no day on which there is no curse, and dew has not come down as a blessing. The good taste of produce is gone."

       F.   R. Yose says, "Also: the fatness of produce is gone."

9:13

       A.   R. Simeon b. Eleazar says, "[When] purity [ceased], it took away the taste and scent; [when] tithes [ceased], they took away the fatness of corn."

       B.   And sages say, "Fornication and witchcraft made an end to everything."

9:14

I.   A.   In the war against Vespasian they decreed against the wearing of wreaths by bridegrooms and against the wedding-drum.

II.   B.   In the war against Titus they decreed against the wearing of wreaths by brides.

       C.   And [they decreed] that a man should not teach Greek to his son.

III.   D.   In the last war [Bar Kokhba's] they decreed that a bride should not go out in a palanquin inside the town.

       E.   But our rabbis [thereafter] permitted the bride to go out in a palanquin inside the town.

9:15

       A.   When R. Meir died, makers of parables came to an end.

       B.   When Ben Azzai died, diligent students came to an end.

       C.   When Ben Zoma died, exegetes came to an end.

       D.   When R. Joshua died, goodness went away from the world.

       E.   When Rabban Simeon b. Gamaliel died, the locust came, and troubles multiplied.

       F.   When R. Eleazar b. Azariah died, wealth went away from the sages.

       G.   When R. Aqiba died, the glory of the Torah came to an end.

       H.   When R. Hanina b. Dosa died, wonder-workers came to an end.

       I.   When R. Yose Qatnuta died, pietists went away.

       J.   (And why was he called <u>Qatnuta</u>? Because he was the least of the pietists.)

       K.   When Rabban Yohanan b. Zakkai died, the splendor of wisdom came to an end.

       L.   When Rabban Gamaliel the Elder died, the glory of the Torah came to an end, and cleanness and separateness perished.

       M.   When R. Ishmael b. Phiabi died, the splendor of the priesthood came to an end.

       N.   When Rabbi died, modesty and fear of sin came to an end.

O. R. Pinhas b. Yair says, "When the Temple was destroyed, associates became ashamed and so did free men, and they covered their heads.

P. "And wonder-workers became feeble. And violent men and big talkers grew strong.

Q. "And none expounds and none seeks [learning] and none asks.

I. R. "Upon whom shall we depend? Upon our Father in heaven."

S. R. Eliezer the Great says, "From the day on which the Temple was destroyed, sages began to be like scribes, and scribes like ministers, and ministers like ordinary folk.

T. "And the ordinary folk have become feeble.

U. "And none seeks.

II. V. "Upon whom shall we depend? Upon our Father in heaven."

W. With the footprints of the Messiah presumption increases, and dearth increases.

X. The vine gives its fruit and wine at great cost.

Y. And the government turns to heresy.

A. And there is no reproof.

AA. The gathering place will be for prostitution.

BB. And Galilee will be laid waste.

CC. And the Gablan will be made desolate.

DD. And the men of the frontier will go about from town to town, and none will take pity on them.

EE. And the wisdom of scribes will putrefy.

FF. And those who fear sin will be rejected.

GG. And the truth will be locked away.

HH. Children will shame elders, and elders will stand up before children.

II. For the son dishonors the father and the daughter rises up against her mother, the daughter-in-law against her mother-in-law; a man's enemies are the men of his own house (Mic. 7:6).

JJ. The face of the generation in the face of a dog.

KK. A son is not ashamed before his father.

III. LL. Upon whom shall we depend? Upon our Father in heaven.

MM. Pinhas b. Yair says, "Heedfulness leads to [hygienic] cleanliness, [hygienic] cleanliness leads to [cultic] cleanness, [cultic] cleanness leads to abstinence, abstinence leads to holiness, holiness leads to modesty, modesty leads to the fear of sin, the fear of sin leads to piety, piety leads to the Holy Spirit, the Holy Spirit leads to the resurrection of the dead, and the resurrection of the dead comes through Elijah, blessed be his memory, Amen."

This is a long and rather complex construction. Concluding the tractate at hand, it is located after a legal passage on the topic of murder. I see the following large, free-standing units: (1) M. Sot. 9:9-12, on the gradual cessation of various rites, with an insertion at M. Sot. 9:10 and an addition at M. Sot. 9:13; (2) M. Sot. 9:14, a triplet appropriately inserted. The melancholy list (3) about how the deaths of various great sages form a counterpart to the decline in the supernatural life of Israel, M. 9:15 A-N, presents a rabbinic counterpart to the cultic construction at the outset. (4) M. 9:15 O-MM is diverse. But the main beam -- the phrase, "Upon whom shall we depend? Upon our Father in heaven" -- does show. It appears to me that M. 9:15 O-R form the bridge, since the theme of the foregoing, the decline of the age marked by the decay of the virtue associated with sages, is carried forward, while the key-phrase in what is to follow is introduced. W-LL then go over the matter yet again.

The Messiah, we notice, occurs rather incidentally and tangentially at M. 9:15W. The important statement is at M. 9:15MM, Pinhas b. Yair's account of the steps toward the end of time. The important fact is that the Messiah does not mark off a rung. Instead Pinhas lays emphasis upon personal virtues, the very virtues any one may master if he keeps the law of the Mishnah, with its interest in particular in cultic cleanness, on the one side, and holiness, on the other. The virtue of each person governs the passage to the resurrection of the dead; everyone is supposed to be modest, fear sin, attain piety. All then are candidates, as potential sages, to receive the Holy Spirit. So far as the Mishnah's pages contain a view of history and a statement of the teleology of the law, it is in this brief statement of Pinhas, and here alone.

The insertion of Elijah as herald of the resurrection of the dead, of course, draws upon the well-known biblical allusion at Malachi 4:5, "Behold, I will send you Elijah the prophet before the great and terrible day of the Lord comes." The Mishnah's authors refer to Elijah as the forerunner of the end at M. Sheq. 2:5, M. B.M. 1:8, 2:8, 3:4-5. His task is defined as settling various disputed questions, in particular involving genealogy (M. Ed. 8:7). Allusion to Elijah here follows what again is a routine convention, established in Scripture, and in no way proposes a revision of it. For the philosophers of the Mishnah the figure of the Messiah presents no rich resource of myth or symbol. The Messiah forms part of the inherited, but essentially undifferentiated, background of factual materials. The figure is neither to be neglected nor to be exploited.

We therefore may hardly find astonishing the failure of the Mishnah's lawyers to pay attention to the possibility of a false Messiah, nor do we even know what sort of Messiah would fall into that classification. The main concern expressed in the law on people we might mislead Israel focuses upon false prophets (M. San. 11:1B, 11:5), and blasphemers (M. San. 7:2S). The principal concern is that people of this sort pose the danger of incitement to idolatry.

Accordingly, the figure of a Messiah at the end of time, coming to save Israel from whatever Israel needs to be saved from, plays a negligible role in the Mishnah's discourse. It follows that fear of the wrong sort of Messiah likewise scarcely comes to the surface. Whether, at M. San. 7:2ff, idolatry or blasphemy in general served to encompass people who might falsely claim to inaugurate the end of time or to do the work of eschatological forgiveness of sins and the ultimate salvation of Israel, no one can say. It seems unlikely.

In all, the Messiah in the Mishnah does not stand at the forefront of the framers' consciousness. The issues encapsulated in the myth and person of the Messiah are scarcely addressed. The framers of the Mishnah do not resort to speculation about the

Messiah as a historical-supernatural figure. So far as that kind of speculation provides the vehicle for reflection on salvific issues, in mythic terms, narratives on the meaning of history and the destiny of Israel, we cannot say that the Mishnah's philosophers take up those encompassing categories of being: Where are we heading? What can we do about it? That does not mean questions found urgent in the aftermath of the destruction of the Temple and the disaster of Bar Kokhba failed to attract the attention of the Mishnah's sages. But they treated history in a different way, offering their own answers to its questions.

iii.   Eschatology without Messiah, Teleology beyond Time

At issue is the direction of eschatology in the foundation-document and its continuations. It is not merely whether, or how frequently, the figures of the Messiah and Elijah make an appearance, how often "the days of the Messiah" come under discussion, or how many references we find to "the end of days" or events we regard as historical. We focus upon how the system laid out in the Mishnah takes up and disposes of those critical issues of teleology worked out through messianic eschatology in other, earlier versions of Judaism. These earlier systems resorted to the myth of the Messiah as savior and redeemer of Israel, a supernatural figure engaged in political-historical tasks as king of the Jews, even a God-man facing the crucial historical questions of Israel's life and resolving them: the Christ as king of the world, of the ages, of death itself. Even though the figure of a Messiah does appear, when the framers of the Mishnah speak of "the Messiah," they mean a high priest designated and consecrated to office in a certain way, and not in some other way. The reference to "days of the Messiah" constitutes a given, a conventional division of history at the end-time but before the ultimate end. But that category of time differentiated plays no consequential role in the teleological framework established within the Mishnah. Accordingly, the Mishnah's framers constructed a system of Judaism in which the entire teleological dimension reached full exposure with scarcely a hint of a need to invoke the person or functions of a Messianic figure of any kind. Perhaps, in the aftermath of Bar Kokhba's debacle, silence on the subject served to express a clarion judgment. I am inclined to think so. But, for the purpose of our inquiry, the main thing is a simple fact, now fully expounded and illustrated.

The issue of eschatology, framed in mythic terms, draws in its wake the issue of how, in the foundation-document of Judaism, history comes to full conceptual expression. History as an account of a meaningful pattern of events, making sense of the past and giving guidance about the future, begins with the necessary conviction that singular events matter, one after another. The Mishnah's framers present us with no elaborate theory of events, a fact fully consonant with their systematic points of insistence and encompassing concern. Events do not matter, one by one. The philosopher-lawyers exhibited no theory of history either. Their conception of Israel's destiny in no way called upon historical categories of either narrative or didactic explanation to describe and account for the future. The small importance attributed to the figure of the Messiah as an historical-eschatological figure, therefore, fully accords with the larger traits of the system as a whole. Let me speak with emphasis: If what is important in Israel's existence is sanctification, an ongoing process, and not salvation, understood as a one-time event at the end, then no one will find reason to narrate history. Few then will form the obsession about the Messiah so characteristic of Judaism in its later, rabbinic mode. But the Messiah then will wear rabbinical cloak and draw Israel to accept the Talmuds' ironic conception of the holy life. Salvation comes through sanctification -- just as M. Sot. 9:15 indicates. Then the salvific figure becomes an instrument of consecration and so fits into a system quite different from one built to begin with around the Messiah in particular.

When, in analyzing the foundations of Judaism, we move from species, eschatology, upward to genus, teleology, we find ourselves addressing head-on the motives and goals of the mishnaic system. The system is so constructed as not to point toward a destination at the end of time. But still it does speak of last things. Accordingly, we ask, where, if not in the eschaton, do things end up? The answer provided by Abot, the Mishnah's first apologetic, is clear: "Where do we head? Where do we go? Below, below, below." Death is the destination. In life we prepare for the voyage. We keep the law in order to make the move required of us all. What is supposed in Abot to make the system work, explaining why we should do the things the Mishnah says, is that other end, the end to which history and national destiny prove remote, or, rather, irrelevant. So, as is clear, Abot constructs a teleology beyond time, providing a purposeful goal for every individual. Life is the antechamber, death, the destination; what we do is weighed and measured. When we die, we stand on one side of the balance, our life and deeds, on the other.

The Mishnah's teleology supplied by Abot presents a curious contrast to the focus of the Mishnah itself. Abot addresses the life of the individual, but only incidentally, the construct of the nation. But the system of the Mishnah, for its part, designs as whole society, one component after another. Mishnaic discourse speaks of the individual in the context of the national life of collective sanctification. Self-evidently, tensions between individual and community reach ready resolution; that is hardly the point. The main thing is that the Mishnah addresses not the stages or phases of individual life, but the constituents of the life of village and Temple, the former shaped, where possible, into the counterpart and mirror image of the latter. To the system of sanctification imagined in the Mishnah, the individual is not a principal building block. The householder and his ménage form the smallest whole unit of social construction. So, as I said, the teleology contributed by Abot to the Mishnaic system turns out to be no more just a fit than the one that might, but did not, come out of Messianic eschatology. Yet the world beyond historical time to which Abot makes reference provides precisely the right metaphysical setting for the system of order and stasis, or proper and correct classification, that underlay, as foundation and goal, the Mishnah's authorities' own detailed statements.

But Judaism at the end did indeed provide an ample account and explanation of Israel's history and destiny. These emerged as the generative problematic of Judaism, just as they framed the social reality confronted by Jews wherever they lived. So, to seek the map that shows the road from the Mishnah, at the beginning, to the fully articulated Judaism of the end of the formative age in late antiquity, we have to look elsewhere. For as to the path from the Mishnah to tractate Abot -- this is not the way.

It could never have been the way because, in my view, the Mishnah with its documents of continuation and succession proposed to ignore the actualities of the social condition of Israel. The critical issues confronting the Jewish nation emerged from its sorry political condition. In the most commonplace sense of the word, these were historical issues. Any sort of Judaism that pretended the history of Israel could be reduced to lists of events sharing the same taxonomic traits, and that the destiny of Israel might be absorbed into an essentially imaginary framework of sanctification attained through the human heart and mind, demanded what the Jewish nation could not give. For people could not pretend to be other than who they were and what they were. Israel constituted a defeated people, driven from its holy place, yet reminded, every time they opened their ancient Scriptures, of God's special love for them and of their distinctive destiny among nations. Israel lived out an insufferable paradox between God's word and world, between promise and postponed fulfillment. So the critical issue confronting any sort of Judaism to emerge in late antiquity reached definition and attained urgency in the social reality, the everyday experience, of Israel: When? By whom? To the Jewish nation history proved very real indeed. The political question of Israel's destiny settled by the myth of the promise of the Messiah's coming salvation -- a concrete, national and historical salvation -- could not be wished away. It demanded response: how long, O Lord? So, as is clear, the Mishnah's system would have to undergo revision and reformation. The labor of renewal would demand fresh and original thinkers: exegetes of a remarkably subtle capacity.

iv.   The Next Stage

The Mishnah, the first document in the canon of formative Judaism, ca. A.D. 200, presented a system of Judaism aimed at the sanctification of Israel. That system invoked a teleology lacking an eschatological dimension. What happened next? The several successive documents of exegesis -- the Talmud of the Land of Israel, the exegetical compositions organized around scriptural books, and the Talmud of Babylonia -- from 400 to 600 then supplied the larger system of formative Judaism, resting upon the constitution of the Mishnah, with that well-established, eschatologically-oriented teleology of Messiah and his salvation that the Mishnah's framers had rejected. The Judaism that emerged was, and now remains, profoundly devoted to questions of history and its meaning, promising salvation attained through holy deeds of eschatological and salvific value. So the Mishnah, a system aimed at sanctification and built upon the mainbeams of nature and supernature, was drawn nearer to the orbit of the on-going everyday life of Israel. The document of a Judaism of sanctification ended up as the foundation of a Judaism of historical salvation. How so? The Talmuds and (in lesser measure) collections of scriptural exegeses presented a system of Judaism focused upon salvation and promising to carry Israel to the age of the coming of the Messiah and the end of history as it was then suffered. Yet, the Messiah in the Talmudic sector of the formative canon emerged as a figure meant to encourage and foster precisely those emphases upon life above time and beyond history, life lived in full acceptance of God's rule in eternity and rejection of man's rule in history, that the Mishnah had originally made the foundation of its system.

Accordingly, when the canon of Judaism had reached the end of its formative period, it presented a version of the Messiah-myth entirely congruent to the character of the foundation-document, the Mishnah. Judaism emerging from late antiquity then would deliver to Israel an enduring message of timeless sanctification, garbed in the cloak of historical, and hence eschatological salvation.

So we here adumbrate the first stage -- the Mishnah's part -- of two reciprocal processes, first the "remessianization" of the canon of formative Judaism, second, the reformation of a Messiah-myth itself to fit into the larger system expressed in that canon. In the end we shall be helped to grasp what is happening if we compare the Messiah in the canon of formative Judaism to the unfolding of the Messiah-myth in the Christian understandings of Jesus as Christ. Early on, Christ, the Messiah, marked the end of history, the expectation of the imminent resurrection of the dead. Later on, the eschatological Messiah would become Jesus: rabbi, teacher, preacher, wonder-worker, God-man, perfect priest, and oblation -- many other things, human and heavenly alike. So the on-going life of the Church turned Christ, the Messiah-Savior at the eschaton, into whatever Christians needed the Christ, Jesus, to be through the eternity of time. The Messiah-myth, originally defined in terms of antecedent, Israelite conventions, entered the grid of Christian being, to be reframed and reformed within that ongoing experience of the enduring "life in Christ." So too, in the formation of Judaism, the eschatological Messiah (so critical to Paul's Christ) was initially rejected as a category useful to the Mishnah's stratum of the canon. The Messiah-myth would then regain pride of place within the Talmuds' sector of the canon. But this was only in terms wholly natural to the points of insistence of the system inaugurated and defined by the Mishnah. So the established conventions, whatever they were, would give way. The Messiah would serve Israel precisely as Israel's rabbis wanted him to -- just as the Messiah would serve the Christian Church as Christians wished. Here, as I said, we have dealt only with the first stage of the process.

v.   The Messianic Idea in Judaism?

The analysis I have given bears some consequences for the methods by which we describe, analyze, and interpret Judaism (or any other religious tradition). Specifically, we must now question those available descriptions, analyses, and interpretations that treat a construct known as "Judaism" and posit "the Judaic idea" about one thing or another. Using as our case the issue of messianic references and themes, we therefore ask whether we may any longer take seriously books under such titles as those of Joseph Klausner, The Messianic Idea in Israel (N.Y., 1955) and Gershom Scholem, The Messianic Idea in Judaism and other essays on Jewish spirituality (N.Y., 1971). In my view books constructed along these lines on the topic at hand constitute little more than composites of texts representative only of the learned authors' capacity to collect texts in a Judaism that existed in fact nowhere, whole and complete, but the authors' imaginations. They are exercises of the free association of things that, in nature, in society, were never associated with one another in just this way, for just this purpose at just this time: pure academic fantasy.

Let me spell this matter out. We find in the Mishnaic sector of the rabbinic canon no such thing as "the Messianic idea," and the rabbinic sources as a whole reveal no such harmonious, encompassing construct. Once we differentiate among stages of a given canon of sources, on the one side, or among types of canonical writings, on the other, we discover formidable distinctions among assertions about the Messiah. More important, we discern diverse ways in which the Messiah-myth serves these several compositions. It follows that we cannot locate the conception of a single prevailing construct, to details of which all assertions about the Messiah by definition testify. When we look at the origins of statements about the Messiah (as about any other topic), we turn out to deconstruct what in fact has been invented whole and complete, in our own time. Klausner and Scholem provide portraits of a composite that, in fact, never existed at any one book, time, or place, or in the imagination of any one social group, except an imagined "Israel." and a made-up "Judaism." How so? Once we distinguish one type or system of Judaism, or one group of Israelites, from another, recognizing commonalities and underscoring points of difference, we no longer find it possible to describe and analyze the Messianic idea at all. Indeed, in the present context, we can no longer even comprehend the parallel categories, the... idea, and in Judaism. The upshot is that a new classification is required, new categories must be defined. These appear, I have shown, in two ways. First, they emerge from the differences between one book and another, related book. Second, they arise from the recognition that categories of books reflect different life-situations. Both of these types of categories form commonplaces in contemporary learning.

We now recognize that the figure of the Messiah serves diverse purposes, defined by the framers of the larger systems in which the Messiah-myth will find a place. We know that the authors of the Mishnah assigned an insubstantial role to the Messiah. But did the framers of the ultimate rabbinical system, in particular the great encyclopaedists of the Talmud of Babylonia, simply open the gate to admit "the Messiah" at large? I think not. What we find in the talmudic sector of the formative canon of Judaism is not merely an established, general conception of the Messiah, now invited to serve (as it supposedly had so well elsewhere) as the principal teleological justification of the rabbinical system. True, the Messiah enters. But he does so only on the rabbis' terms. So he is incorporated into the rabbinical realm through a process of assimilation and (from the viewpoint I think dominant among the Mishnah's philosophers) also neutralization.

Under the circumstances, it is difficult to see that the rabbis had much choice. The vivid expectation of the imminent advent of the Messiah could hardly continue indefinitely. For instance, decades after Paul's declarations on that matter, people were still dying, the assembled people of God still suffering, as the Gospels' authors realized. So the Messiah had to find secondary, long-term embodiment in some form: rabbi, priest, master and divine model on earth -- God-with-us, the word made flesh, Son of Man in the image of God -- and in heaven, yet other tasks. So the ahistorical Christ of Paul, lacking all biography, becomes the Jesus of Q, Matthew, Mark, and Luke, ends up as the Jesus Christ of John and of everyone beyond: no longer merely the celebrant of the end of time, but now the center and pivot of all time, all being, all history. Shall we then conclude that the established, inherited conception of the Messiah, as termination of life and time, defined for the heirs and continuators of Christ in the church what they would see in him and say about him? Quite to the contrary. They inherited, but also reshaped the inheritance. Whatever happened in the beginning, Christ as Messiah continued to serve, long after the moment that should have marked the end of time. Now as the ever-stable focus and pivot of Christian existence, the Messiah became something other and far more useful. So far as the apocalyptic expectations were not realized, indeed, could not have been realized, the Messiah had to become something else than what people originally expected. True, he will still be called Christ. But he will be whatever the Church needs him to be: anything but terminus of a world history that -- up to now -- refuses to come to an end.

So too was the case of the Messiah in the formative canon of Judaism. That is, if we take for granted that people to begin with imagined the Messiah in accordance with the promises of old, we must assume that at the outset they saw the Messiah as an apocalyptic figure, coming at the end of time. As dominant and definitive pattern, that version of the Messiah-myth then passed from the center of the stage of the Messiah. Other patterns -- attempts to explain the same unclassifiable figure -- came into use. As to the Mishnah's part of the canon, at the beginning the authors wished, so far as possible, to avoid all reliance upon the Messiah as apocalyptic figure. Even the language was given a meaning not primary in the prior writings, "messiah" as (mere) high priest, "messiah" as something other than eschatological savior, whether priest or general, whether from David's line or the house of Joseph. But then in the Talmuds' sector of the canon, the figure of the Messiah, and the concerns addressed through discourse about that figure, came to the fore in powerful expression. So, to state my thesis briefly and with emphasis: (1) Established conventions of the Messiah-myth served the Church merely to classify Jesus at the outset, but later on, other taxa came into play. (2) The Messiah-myth found no consequential place in the rabbinical canon at the outset, that is, in the Mishnah, but later on that same myth became the moving force, the principal mode of teleological thought in the Talmudic sector.

If I had to guess why the Talmuds gave prominence to a concept ignored in the Mishnah, I should have to appeal to the evidence of what the nation, Israel at large, had long had in mind. It seems to me self-evident that a Judaism lacking an eschatological dimension must have contradicted two established facts. First, the people read Scripture, which told them about the end of days. Second, the condition of the people, deteriorating as it was, called into question the credibility of the ahistorical construction of the Mishnah. So, I should imagine, for the Mishnah to be of any practical use, it required not only application to diverse circumstances, which the rabbis gave it. Its system also required expansion, not only by augmenting what was there, but also by exploring dimensions not contained therein at all. By reshaping the teleology of the mishnaic system into an eschatological idiom -- indeed, by restating the eschatology in the established Messianic myth -- the rabbis of the Talmud made the Mishnah's system over.

But if the Mishnah was thus forced into that very grid of history and eschatology that it had been formulated to reject, the Mishnah's mode in turn drastically modified the Messiah-myth. For the latter was recast into the philosophical mode of thought and stated as teleology of an eternally-present sanctification attained by obedience to patterns of holiness laid out in the Torah. This grid is precisely the one that the framers of the Mishnah had defined. So by no means may we conclude that what changed, in the end, was the Mishnah's system. Its modes of thought intact, its fundamental points of insistence about Israel's social policy reaffirmed, the Mishnah's system ended up wholly definitive for Judaism as it emerged in the canon at the end of its formative centuries, the "one whole Torah of Moses, our rabbi."

How so? The version of the Messiah-myth incorporated into the rabbinic system through the Talmuds simply restates the obvious: Israel's sanctification is what governs. So if Israel will keep a single Sabbath (or two in succession), the Messiah will come. If Israel stops violating the Torah, the Messiah will come. If Israel acts with arrogance in rejecting its divinely-assigned condition, the Messiah will not come. Everything depends, then, upon the here-and-now of everyday life. The operative category is not salvation through what Israel does, but sanctification of what Israel is. The fundamental convictions of the Mishnah's framers, flowing from the reaction against the apocalyptic and messianic wars of the late first and early second centuries, here absorbed and redirected precisely those explosive energies that, to begin with, had made Israel's salvation through history the critical concern. So while the Talmuds introduced a formerly neglected myth, in fact in their version the Messiah became precisely what the sages of the Mishnah and their continuators in the Talmud most needed: a rabbi-Messiah, who will save an Israel sanctified through Torah. Salvation then depends upon sanctification, so is subordinated to it.

The Mishnah then, proposed to build an Israelite world view and way of life that ignored the immediate apocalyptic and historical terrors of the age. The Mishnah's heirs and continuators, who produced the other sector of the formative canon, did two things. They preserved that original policy for Israelite society. But they also accommodated an ongoing social and psychological reality: the presence of terror, the foreboding of doom, and Israel's iron-clad faith in the God who saves. Israel remained the old Israel of history, suffering, and hope. The Mishnah's fantasy of an Israel beyond time, an Israel living in nature and supernature, faded away. It was implausible. The facts of history contradicted it.

Yet Israel's condition, moral and social, must govern Israel's destiny -- in accordance with the Torah's rules, but also precisely as biblical prophecy and Mishnaic doctrine had claimed. What then could Israel do about its own condition? How could Israel confront the unending apocalypse of its own history? Israel could do absolutely nothing. But Israel could be -- become -- holy. That is why history was relegated to insignificance. Humble acceptance of the harsh rule of gentiles would render Israel worthy of God's sudden intervention, the institution of God's rule through King-Messiah.

Under the circumstances of Israel from that day almost down to our own time, that counsel proved not only good theology but also astute social policy. Until our own time the nations did not oppress Israel "too much," Israel did not rebel "too soon." What the rabbinic canon set forth at the end, in its rich eschatological-messianic myth and symbolism, states precisely what the Mishnah at the outset had defined as its teleology, but in the idiom of life and death, nature and supernature. The rabbinical canon in its ultimate form delivered the message of sanctification, garbed in the language of salvation -- but not garbled by that expression. So diverse systems of Judaism make use of messianic materials to make their own statements. In the case of the Messiah-theme in the Mishnah's successor-documents, if the hands are the hands of the inherited eschatological faith of prophecy and apocalypse, the voice remains the true voice of Jacob, that is, speaking through the Mishnah.

Chapter Four

BEYOND MYTH, AFTER APOCALYPSE:
THE MISHNAIC CONCEPTION OF HISTORY

i.   Why the Mishnah Differs

The framers of the Mishnah, a late second century law code, which along with the Hebrew Bible, forms the foundation of Judaism as we know it, present us with a kind of historical thinking quite different from the one they, along with all Israel, had inherited in Scripture. The legacy of prophecy, apocalypse, and mythic-history ("Heilsgeschichte") handed on by the writers of the books of the Old Testament exhibits a single and quite familiar conception of history seen whole. Events bear meaning, God's message and judgment. What happens is singular, therefore, an event to be noted, and points toward lessons to be drawn for where things are heading and why. If things do not happen at random, they also do not form indifferent patterns of merely secular, social facts. What happens is important because of the meaning contained therein. That meaning is to be discovered and revealed through the narrative of what has happened.

So for all forms of Judaism until the Mishnah, the writing of history serves as a form of prophecy. Just as prophecy takes up the interpretation of historical events, so historians retell these events in the frame of prophetic theses. And out of the two -- historiography as a mode of mythic reflection, prophecy as a means of mythic construction -- emerges a picture of future history, that is, what is going to happen. That picture, framed in terms of visions and supernatural symbols, in the end focuses, as much as do prophecy and history-writing, upon the here and now.

The upshot is simple. History consists of a sequence of one-time events, each singular, all meaningful. These events move from a beginning somewhere to an end at a foreordained goal. History moves toward eschatology, the end of history. The teleology of Israel's life finds its definition in eschatological fulfillment. Eschatology therefore constitutes not a choice within teleology, but a definition of teleology. History done in this way then sits enthroned as the queen of theological science. Events do not conform to patterns. They form patterns. What happens matters because events bear meaning, constitute history.

Now, as is clear, such a conception of mythic and apocalyptic history comes to realization in the writing of history in the prophetic pattern or in the apocalyptic framework, both of them mythic modes of organizing events. We have every right to expect such a view of matters to lead people to write books of a certain sort, rather than of some other. In the case of Judaism, obviously, we should expect people to write history books that teach lessons or apocalyptic books that through pregnant imagery predict the future and record the direction and end of time. And in antiquity that kind of writing proves commonplace among all kinds of groups and characteristic of all sorts of Judaisms but one.

The Mishnah, which I have identified in the preceding chapter, contains a very few tales, and no large-scale conception of history. It organizes its system in non-historical and socially unspecific terms, lacking all precedent in prior systems of Judaism or in prior kinds of Judaic literature. Instead of narrative, it gives description of how things are done, that is, descriptive laws. Instead of reflection on the meaning and end of history, it constructs a world in which history plays little part. Instead of narratives full of didactic meaning, it provides lists of events so as to expose the traits that they share and thus the rules to which they conform. The definitive components of a historical-eschatological system of Judaism -- description of events as one time happenings, analysis of the meaning and end of events, and interpretation of the end and future of singular events -- none of these commonplace constituents of all other systems of Judaism (including nascent Christianity) of ancient times finds a place in the Mishnah's system of Judaism.

So, as we shall see, the Mishnah finds no precedent in prior Israelite writings for its mode of dealing with things that happen. The Mishnah's way of identifying happenings as consequential and describing them, its way of analyzing those events it chooses as bearing meaning, its interpretation of the future to which significant events point -- all those in context were unique. Yet to say that the Mishnah's system is ahistorical could not be more wrong. The Mishnah presents a different kind of history. More to the point, it revises the inherited conception of history and reshapes that conception to fit into its own system. When we consider the power of the biblical myth, the force of its eschatological and messianic interpretation of history, the effect of apocalypse, we must find astonishing the capacity of the Mishnah's framers to think in a different way about the same things. As teleology constructed outside the eschatological mode of thought in the setting of the biblical world of ancient Israel proves amazing. Let me now show some of the principal texts that contain and convey this other conception of how events become history and how history teaches lessons.

ii.   The Uses and Meaning of History in the Mishnah

By "history" I mean not merely events, but how events are so organized and narrated as to teach lessons, reveal patterns, tell us what we must do and why, what will happen to us tomorrow. In that context, some events contain richer lessons than others; the destruction of the Temple of Jerusalem teaches more than a crop failure, being kidnapped into slavery more than stubbing one's toe. Furthermore, lessons taught by events -- "history" in the didactic sense -- follow a progression from trivial and private to consequential and public. The framers of the Mishnah explicitly refer to very few events, treating those they do mention within a focus quite separate from what happened -- the unfolding of the events themselves. They rarely create or use narratives. More probative still, historical events do not supply organizing categories or taxonomic classifications. We find no tractate devoted to the destruction of the Temple, no complete chapter detailing the events of Bar Kokhba, nor even a sustained celebration of the events of the sages' own historical life. When things that have happened are mentioned, it is neither in order to narrate, nor to interpret and draw lessons from, the event. It is either to illustrate a point of law or to pose a problem of the law -- always _en passent_, never in a pointed way.

So when sages refer to what has happened, this is casual and tangential to the main thrust of discourse. For example, the "men slain at Tel Arza" (by the Romans?) come under discussion only because we have to decide whether they are to be declared legally dead so their wives may remarry (M. Yebamot 16:7). The advent of gentiles to Jerusalem (in 70?) raises the question of whether we assume a priest's wife has been raped (M. Ketubot 2:9). A war comes into sight -- not named, not important -- only because of a queen's vow, taken when her son goes off "to war" (M. Nazir 4:1). Famous events, of enduring meaning, such as the return to Zion from Babylonia in the time of Ezra and Nehemiah, gain entry into the Mishnah's discourse only because of the genealogical divisions of Israelite society into castes among the immigrants (M. Qiddushin 4:1). Where the Mishnah provides little tales or narratives, moreover, they more often treat how things in the cult are done in general than what, in particular, happened on some one day. For instance, there is the tale of the burning of the red cow (M. Parah Chapter three) or of the purification of the mesora of Lev. 13:2ff. (M. Negaim Chapter Fourteen). The names of Temple officers are catalogued (M. Sheqalim 51:1). But we learn no more about them than the jobs to which they were assigned. Allusions to famous events even within sages' own circles do not demand detailed narration (as to M. Kelim 5:10). It is sufficient to refer casually to well-known incidents. Narrative, in the Mishnah's limited rhetorical repertoire, is reserved for the narrow framework of what priests and others do on recurrent occasions and around the Temple. In all, that staple of history, stories about dramatic events and important deeds, in the minds of the Mishnah's jurisprudents provide little nourishment. Events, if they appear at all, are treated as trivial. They may be well-known, but are consequential in some way other than is revealed in the detailed account of what actually happened.

Sages' treatment of events, as we shall now see in detail, determines what in the Mishnah is important about what happens. Since the greatest event in the century and a half, from ca. A.D. 50 to ca. 200, in which the Mishnah's materials came into being, was the destruction of the Temple in A.D. 70, we must expect the Mishnah's treatment of that incident to illustrate the document's larger theory of history: what is important and unimportant about what happens. The treatment of the destruction occurs in two ways.

First, the destruction of the Temple constitutes a noteworthy fact in the history of the law. Why? Because various laws about rite and cult had to undergo revision on account of the destruction. The following provides a stunningly apt example of how the Mishnah's philosophers regard what actually happened as being simply changes in the law:

M. Rosh Hashanah 4:1-4

4:1

A.   On the festival day of the New Year which coincided with the Sabbath --

B.   in the Temple they would sound the shofar.

C.   But not in the provinces.

D.   When the Temple was destroyed, Rabban Yohanan ben Zakkai made the rule that they should sound the shofar in every locale in which there was a court.

E.   Said R. Eleazar, "Rabban Yohanan b. Zakkai made that rule in the case of Yabneh
      alone."

F.   They said to him, "All the same are Yabneh and every locale in which there is a
      court."

4:2

A.   And in this regard also was Jerusalem ahead of Yabneh:

B.   in every town which is within sight and sound [of Jerusalem], and nearby and able to
      come to Jerusalem, they sound the shofar.

C.   But as to Yabneh, they sound the shofar only in the court alone.

4:3

A.   In olden times the lulab was taken up in the Temple for seven days, and in the
      provinces for one day.

B.   When the Temple was destroyed, Rabban Yohanan ben Zakkai made the rule that in
      the provinces the lulab should be taken up for seven days, as a memorial to the
      Temple;

C.   and that the day [the sixteenth of Nisan] on which the omer is waved should be
      wholly prohibited [in regard to the eating of new produce] (M. Suk. 3:12).

4:4

A.   At first they would receive testimony about the new moon all day long.

B.   One time the witnesses came late, and the Levites consequently were mixed up as to
      [what] song [they should sing].

C.   They made the rule that they should receive testimony [about the new moon] only up
      to the afternoon offering.

D.   Then, if witnesses came after the afternoon-offering, they would treat that entire
      day as holy, and the next day as holy too.

E.   When the Temple was destroyed, Rabban Yohanan b. Zakkai made the rule that they
      should [once more] receive testimony about the new moon all day long.

F.   Said R. Joshua b. Qorha, "This rule too did Rabban Yohanan B. Zakkai make:

G.   "Even if the head of the court is located somewhere else, the witnesses should come
      only to the location of the council [to give testimony, and not to the location of the
      head of the court]."

The passages before us leave no doubt about what sages selected as important about the
destruction: it produced changes in synagogue rites.

      Second, although the sages surely mourned for the destruction and the loss of
Israel's principal mode of worship, and certainly recorded the event of the ninth of Ab in
the year A.D. 70, they did so in their characteristic way: they listed the event as an item
in a catalogue of things that are like one another and so demand the same response.

      But then the destruction no longer appears as a unique event. It is absorbed into a
pattern of like disasters, all exhibiting similar taxonomic traits, events to which the
people, now well-schooled in tragedy, knows full well the appropriate response. So it is in
demonstrating regularity that sages reveal their way of coping. Then the uniqueness of
the event fades away, its mundane character is emphasized. The power of taxonomy in

imposing order upon chaos once more does its healing work. The consequence was reassurance that historical events obeyed discoverable laws. Israel's ongoing life would override disruptive, one-time happenings. So catalogues of events, as much as lists of species of melons, served as brilliant apologetic by providing reassurance that nothing lies beyond the range and power of ordering system and stabilizing pattern.

<u>M. Taanit 4:6-7</u>

<u>4:6</u>

A. Five events took place for our fathers on the seventeenth of Tammuz, and five on the ninth of Ab.

B. On the seventeenth of Tammuz (1) the tablets [of the Torah] were broken, (2) the daily whole offering was cancelled, (3) the city wall was breached, (4) Apostemos burned the Torah, and (5) he set up an idol in the Temple.

C. On the ninth of Ab (1) the decree was made against our forefathers that they should not enter the land, (2) the first Temple and (3) the second [Temple] were destroyed, (4) Betar was taken, and (5) the city was ploughed up [after the war of Hadrian].

D. When Ab comes, rejoicing diminishes.

<u>4:7</u>

A. In the week in which the ninth of Ab occurs it is prohibited to get a haircut and to wash one's clothes.

B. But on Thursday of that week these are permitted,

C. because of the honor due to the Sabbath.

D. On the eve of the ninth of Ab a person should not eat two prepared dishes, nor should one eat meat or drink wine.

E. Rabban Simeon b. Gamaliel says, "He should make some change from ordinary procedures."

F. R. Judah declares people obligated to turn over beds.

G. But sages did not concur with him.

I include M. Taanit 4:7 to show the context in which the list of M. 4:6 stands. The stunning calamities catalogued at M. 4:6 form groups, reveal common traits, so are subject to classification. Then the laws of M. 4:7 provide regular rules for responding to, coping with, these untimely catastrophes, all (fortuitously) in a single classification. So the raw materials of history are absorbed into the ahistorical, supernatural system of the Mishnah. The process of absorption and regularization of the unique and one-time moment is illustrated in the passage at hand.

Along these same lines, the entire history of the cult, so critical in the larger system created by the Mishnah's lawyers, produced a patterned, therefore sensible and intelligible, picture. As is clear, everything that happened turned out to be susceptible of classification, once the taxonomic traits were specified. A monothetic exercise, sorting out periods and their characteristics, took the place of narrative, to explain things in its own way: first this, and then that, and, in consequence, the other. So in the neutral turf of holy ground, as much as in the trembling earth of the Temple mount, everything was absorbed into one thing, all classified in its proper place and by its appropriate rule. Indeed, so far as the lawyers proposed to write history at all, they wrote it into their picture of the long tale of the way in which Israel served God: the places in which the sacrificial labor was carried on, the people who did it, the places in which the priests ate the meat left over for their portion after God's portion was set aside and burned up. This "historical" account forthwith generated precisely that problem of locating the regular and orderly, which the philosophers loved to investigate: the intersection of conflicting by equally correct taxonomic rules, as we see at M. Zebahim 14:9, below. The passage that follows therefore is history, so far as the Mishnah's creators proposed to write history: the reduction of events to rules forming compositions of regularity, therefore meaning:

<u>M. Zebahim 14:4-8+9</u>

<u>14:4</u>

I.   A.   Before the tabernacle was set up, (1) the high places were permitted, and (2) [the sacrificial] service [was done by] the first born [Num. 3:12-13, 8:16-18].

    B.   When the tabernacle was set up, (1) the high places were prohibited, and (2) the [sacrificial] service [was done by] priests.

    C.   Most Holy Things were eaten within the veils, Lesser Holy Things [were eaten] throughout the camp of Israel.

<u>14:5</u>

II.   A.   They came to Gilgal.

    B.   The High places were permitted.

    C.   Most Holy Things were eaten within the veils, Lesser Holy Things, anywhere.

<u>14:6</u>

III.   A.   They came to Shiloh.

    B.   The high places were prohibited.

    C.   (1) There was no roof-beam there, but below was a house of stone, and hangings above it, and (2) it was "the resting place" [Deut. 12:0].

    D.   Most Holy Things were eaten within the veils, Lesser Holy Things and second-tithe [were eaten] in any place within sight [of Shiloh].

<u>14:7</u>

IV.   A.   They came to Nob and Gibeon.

    B.   The high places were permitted.

    C.   Most Holy Things were eaten within the veils, Lesser Holy Things, in all the towns of Israel.

<u>14:8</u>

V.   A.   They came to Jerusalem.

    B.   The high places were prohibited.

    C.   And they never again were permitted.

    D.   And it was "the inheritance" [Deut. 12:9].

    E.   Most Holy things were eaten within the veils, Lesser Holy Things and second-tithe within the wall.

14:9

A.   All the Holy things which one sanctified at the time of the prohibition of the high places and offered at the time of the prohibition of the high places outside --

B.   lo, these are subject to the transgression of a positive commandment and a negative commandment, and they are liable on their account to extirpation [for sacrificing outside the designated place, Lev. 17:8-9, M. Zeb. 13:1A].

C.   [If] one sanctified them at the time of the permission of high places and offered them up at the time of the prohibition of high places,

D.   lo, these are subject to transgression of a positive commandment and to a negative commandment, but they are not liable on their account to extirpation [since if the offerings had been sacrificed when they were sanctified, there should have been no violation].

E.   [If] one sanctified them at the time of the prohibition of high places and offered them up at the time of the permission of high places,

F.   lo, these are subject to transgression of a positive commandment, but they are not subject to a negative commandment at all.

The inclusion of M. Zeb. 14:9, structurally matching M. Taanit 4:7, shows us the goal of the historical composition. It is to set forth rules that intersect and produce confusion, so that we may sort out confusion and make sense of all the data.

The upshot may now be stated briefly. The Mishnah absorbs into its encompassing system all events, small and large. With what happens the sages accomplish what they do with everything else: a vast labor of taxonomy, an immense construction of the order and rules governing the classification of everything on earth and in Heaven. The disruptive character of history -- one-time events of ineluctable significance -- scarcely impresses the philosophers. They find no difficulty in showing that what appears unique and beyond classification has in fact happened before and so falls within the range of trustworthy rules and known procedures. Once history's components, one-time events, lose their distinctiveness, then history as a didactic intellectual construct, as a source of lessons and rules, also loses all pertinence.

So lessons and rules come from sorting things out and classifying them, that is, from the procedures and modes of thought of the philosopher seeking regularity. To this labor of taxonomy, the historian's way of selecting data and arranging them into patterns of meaning to teach lessons, proves inconsequential. One-time events are not what matters. The world is composed of nature and supernature. The repetitious laws that count are those to be discovered in Heaven and, in Heaven's creation and counterpart, on earth. Keep those laws and things will work out. Break them, and the result is predictable: calamity of whatever sort will supervene in accordance with the rules. But just because it is predictable, a catastrophic happening testifies to what has always been and must always be, in accordance with reliable rules and within categories already discovered and well explained. That is why the lawyer-philosophers of the mid-second century produced the Mishnah -- to explain how things are. Within the framework of well-classified rules, there could be messiahs, but no single Messiah (in Christian theological terms: <u>Geschichte</u>, but no <u>Historie</u>).

Up to now I have contrasted "history" with "eternity," and framed matters in such a way that the Mishnah's system appears to have been ahistorical and anti-historical. Yet in fact the framers of the Mishnah recognized the past-ness of the past and hence, by definition, laid out a conception of the past that constitutes a historical doctrine. But it is a different conception from the familiar one. To express the difference, I point out that, for modern history-writing, what is important is to describe what is unique and individual, not what is on-going and unremarkable.

<u>History is the story of change, development, movement, not of what does not change, develop, or move. For the thinkers of the Mishnah, historical patterning emerges as today scientific knowledge does, through taxonomy, the classification of the unique and individual, the organization of change and movement within unchanging categories.</u>

That is why the dichotomy between history and eternity, change and permanence, signals an unnuanced exegesis of what was, in fact, a subtle and reflective doctrine of history. That doctrine proves entirely consistent with the large perspectives of scribes, from the ones who made omen-series in ancient Babylonia to the ones who made the Mishnah. That is why the category of salvation does not serve, but the one of sanctification fits admirably.

iii.   Mishnah's Complement: Apocalypse in Tosefta

Sometime between 200 and 400 a corpus of materials in the language and style of the Mishnah was collected to complement the teachings of the Mishnah. This corpus, the Tosefta, was framed in the same period as the founding of the two great Talmuds, one of the Land of Israel, the other of Babylonia. But it adhered closely to the modes of organization and of thought of the Mishnah, and hence serves as a suitable answer to the question: what happened next? For there are two answers, the one at hand, the other in the two Talmuds. A separate account of the latter is required. But the Tosefta's collectors organized and expressed information just as did those of the Mishnah, and they did so in order to say pretty much the same things. That is why it is appropriate to conclude this account of the Mishnah by taking one step outward and beyond.

We close our inquiry with a stunning example of how, in the Tosefta, the system constructed by the founders of the Mishnah treats already-available historical-apocalyptic materials of Scripture. The passage at hand, familiar from my earlier discussion, shows us what the Tosefta's authorities, sometime a century after the Mishnah, do with the most historical of all scriptural materials: apocalypse. The climax of scriptural historiography comes in apocalyptic interpretations of natural symbols in terms of concrete historical events, and of events in terms of symbols. Such interpretation is provided by the visionaries in the book of Daniel. To appreciate the Mishnah's power, we see the Tosefta's transformation of the apocalyptic vision, following the entire discussion in context. What we see is the interpretation of the apocalyptic vision of history wholly in terms of what happens within the circles of sages' debates -- a truly stunning metamorphosis out of history entirely and into the realm of philosophers:

T. Miqvaot 7:11

A. A cow which drank purification-water, and which one slaughtered within twenty-four hours --

B. This was a case, and R. Yose the Galilean did declare it clean, and R. Aqiba did declare it unclean.

C. R. Tarfon supported R. Yose the Galilean. R. Simeon ben Nanos supported R. Aqiba.

D. R. Simeon b. Nanos dismissed [the arguments of] R. Tarfon. R. Yose the Galilean dismissed [the arguments of] R. Simeon b. Nanos.

E. R. Aqiba dismissed [the arguments of] R. Yose the Galilean.

F. After a time, he [Yose] found an answer for him [Aqiba].

G. He said to him, "Am I able to reverse myself?"

H. He said to him, "Not anyone [may reverse himself], but you [may do so], for you are Yose the Galilean."

I. [He said to him,] "I shall say to you: Lo, Scripture states, And they shall be kept for the congregation of the people of Israel for the water for impurity (Num. 19:9).

J. "Just so long as they are kept, lo, they are water for impurity -- but not after a cow has drunk them."

K. This was a case, and thirty-two elders voted in Lud and declared it clean.

L. At that time R. Tarfon recited this verse:

M. "I saw the ram goring westward and northward and southward, and all the animals were unable to stand against it, and none afforded protection from its power, and it did just as it liked and grew great (Dan. 8:4) --

N. "[This is] R. Aqiba.

O. "'As I was considering, behold, a he-goat came from the west across the face of the whole earth, without touching the ground; and the goat had a conspicuous horn between his eyes.

P. "'He came to the ram with the two horns, which I had seen standing on the bank of the river, and he ran at him in his mighty wrath. I saw him come close to the ram, and he was enraged against him and struck the ram and broke his two horns' -- this is R. Aqiba and R. Simeon b. Nanos.

Q. "'And the ram had no power to stand before him' -- this is R. Aqiba.

R. "'But he cast him down to the ground and trampled upon him' -- this is R. Yose the Galilean.

S. "'And there was no one who could rescue the ram from his power' -- these are the thirty two elders who voted in Lud and declared it clean."

In the sages' debates Daniel's vision of the kingdoms now is turned into an account of the class of titans. The history of nations, their wars and kings and victories, moves from the world of material reality to the realm of mind constructed in the fantastic law systems of the Mishnah and the Tosefta. History in the ordinary sense of the word is not merely rejected or ignored. It is transformed. The process inaugurated in the Mishnah's reduction of unique events to their monothetic taxa and absorption of these events within a system of predictable classification here reaches its climax. People who know what history really consists of will then recognize that sages make history. They make history in the thoughts they think and the rules they lay down. In such a context as this, there is place for neither history nor an end of history, nor will the Messiah find his services required.

iv.   Sanctification and Teleology

The issue of eschatology, framed in mythic terms, draws in its wake the issue of how, in the Mishnah as the foundation-document of Judaism, history comes to full conceptual expression. History as an account of a meaningful pattern of events, making sense of the past and giving guidance about the future, begins with the necessary conviction that events matter, one after another. The Mishnah's framers present us with no elaborate theory of events, a fact fully consonant with their systematic points of insistence and encompassing concern. Events do not matter, one by one. The philosopher-lawyers exhibited no theory of history either. Their conception of Israel's destiny in no way called upon historical categories of either narrative or didactic explanation to describe and account for the future. The small importance attributed to the figure of the Messiah as an historical-eschatological figure, therefore, fully accords with the larger traits of the system as a whole. Let me speak with emphasis: If what is important in Israel's existence is sanctification, an ongoing process, and not salvation, understood as a one-time event at the end, then no one will find reason to narrate history.

That is why, at the end, we come to the absurdity of the reduction of an apocalyptic vision of the wars of great empires to the paltry dimensions of an academic argument about nothing of material consequence. Were it not for the document's prevailing seriousness, we might be inclined to see Tarfon's reading of Daniel 8:4 as a remarkably subtle and ironic judgment: a joke. But, so far as I know, it was not a joke. The disproportion between Daniel's images asnd Tarfon's interpretation strikes us. But it struck no one before us. What we learn from the Tosefta is the way forward, from the Mishnah onward, as it was explored by some in the third and fourth centuries. So, as I said, the Tosefta tells us what people might have done.

But, we realize full well, the Tosefta does not point toward the character of Judaism as it was to emerge from late antiquity: richly eschatological, obsessed with the Messiah and his coming, engaged by the history of Israel and the nations. The Tosefta, in line with the Mishnah, allowed no glimpse at a doctrine of Israel's history and destiny, because the framers had nothing to show. But Judaism at the end did indeed provide an ample account and explanation of Israel's history and destiny. These emerged as the generative problematic of Judaism, just as they framed the social reality confronted by Jews wherever they lived. So, to seek the map that shows the road from the Mishnah, at the beginning, to the fully articulated Judaism of the end of the formative age in late antiquity, we have to look elsewhere. For as to the path from the Mishnah through the Tosefta -- this is not the way people took.

Chapter Five

MESSIAH REDIVIVUS:

THE CONCEPTION OF HISTORY IN THE TALMUD OF THE LAND OF ISRAEL

The Mishnah describes a world and presents rules for it. So we may say, in simple language, that the Mishnah is about "life." The Mishnah describes the life of Israel, viewed from one perspective. But the Talmud of the Land of Israel, for its part, is not so much about "life" in general as it is about the Mishnah in particular. Whatever the framers of the Talmud's units of discourse wish to say, they choose to say generally in relationship to something they find in the Mishnah. The Talmud nonetheless follows a distinctive program of topics. At issue here is that which the Mishnah does not choose to treat, but the Talmud for its part wishes to discuss. I refer to the absence in the Mishnah of a taxon defined by the issue of Israel's history, its form, direction, meaning, and end. These fall wholly outside of the Mishnah's frame of reference. On the protean topic, the Mishnah offers no tractate, no chapter, scarcely a reference. Not only do we find no attention to that classical issue of the Israelite world-view, we do not even know how we might find appropriate, specifically Mishnaic, language or categories for discussion of the issue. Suitable words elude us. Whatever discourse we do find in the Talmud pertinent to this formidable and urgent topic therefore lies wholly outside the symbolic and even linguistic-conceptual framework of the Mishnah. As a result, it is principally when the Talmud ignores the Mishnah that it addresses questions important to the present inquiry.

i.   The Uses and Meaning of History in the Talmud of the Land of Israel.

Disorderly historical events entered the system of the Mishnah and found their place within the larger framework of the Mishnah's orderly world. So to claim that the Mishnah's framers merely ignored what was happening would be incorrect. They worked out their own way of dealing with historical events, the disruptive power of which they not only conceded but freely recognized. Further, the Mishnah's authors to begin with did not intend to compose a history book or a work of prophecy or apocalypse. Even if they had wanted to narrate the course of events, they could hardly have done so through the medium of the Mishnah. Yet the Mishnah presents its philosophy in full awareness of the issues of historical calamity confronting the Jewish nation. So far as the philosophy of the document confronts the totality of Israel's existence, the Mishnah by definition _also_ presents a philosophy of history.

The Mishnah's subordination of historical events contradicts the emphasis of a thousand years of Israelite thought. The biblical histories, the ancient prophets, the apocalyptic visionaries -- all had testified that what happened mattered. Events carried the message of the living God. That is, events constituted history, pointed toward, and so

- 67 -

explained, Israel's destiny. An essentially ahistorical system of timeless sanctification, worked out through construction of an eternal rhythm centered on the movement of the moon and stars and seasons, represented a choice taken by few outside of the priesthood. Furthermore, the pretense that what happens matters less than what is testified against palpable and remembered reality. For Israel had suffered enormous loss of life. As we shall see, the Talmud of the Land of Israel takes these events seriously and treats them as unique and remarkable. The memories proved real. The hopes evoked by the Mishnah's promise of sanctification of the world in static perfection did not. For they had to compete with the grief of an entire century of mourning:

Y. Taanit 4:5

X. B. Rabbi would derive by exegesis twenty-four tragic events from the verse: "The Lord has destroyed without mercy all the habitation of Jacob; in his wrath he has broken down the strongholds of the daughter of Judah; he has brought down to the ground in dishonor the kingdom and its rulers" (Lam. 2:2).

C. R. Yohanan derived sixty from the same verse.

D. Did R. Yohanan then find more than did Rabbi in the same verse?

E. But because Rabbi lived nearer to the destruction of the Temple, there were in the audience old men who remembered what had happened, and when he gave his exegesis, they would weep and fall silent and get up and leave.

We do not know whether things happened as the story-teller says. But the fact remains that the framers of the Yerushalmi preserved the observation that, in Rabbi's time, memories of world-shaking events continued to shape Israel's mind and imagination. For people like those portrayed here, the Mishnah's taxonomic classification of tragedy to accord with trustworthy rules cannot have solved many problems.

Accordingly, we should not be surprised to observe that the Talmud of the Land of Israel contains evidence pointing toward substantial steps taken in rabbinical circles, away from the position of the Mishnah. We find materials that fall entirely outside the framework of historical doctrine established within the Mishnah. These are, first, an interest in the periodization of history, and second, a willingness to include events of far greater diversity than those in the Mishnah. So the Yerushalmi contains an expanded view of the range of human life encompassed to begin with by the conception of history.

Let us take the second point first. So far as things happen that demand attention and so constitute "events," within the Mishnah these fall into two classifications: (1) biblical history, and (2) events involving the Temple. A glance at the catalogue, cited above from M. Ta. 4:6, tells us what kind of happening constitutes an "event," a historical datum demanding attention and interpretation. In the Talmud at hand, by contrast, in addition to Temple-events, we find also two other sorts of Geschichten: Torah-events, that is, important stories about the legal and supernatural doings of rabbis, and also political events.

These events, moreover, involved people not considered in the Mishnah: gentiles as much as Jews, Rome as much as Israel. The Mishnah's history, such as it is, knows only

Israel. The Talmud greatly expands the range of historical interest when it develops a theory of Rome's relationship to Israel and, of necessity also, Israel's relationship to Rome.

Only by taking account of the world at large can the Talmud's theory of history yield a philosophy of history worthy of the name, that is, an account of who Israel is, the meaning of what happens to Israel, and the destiny of Israel in this world and at the end of time. Israel by itself -- as the priests had claimed -- lived in eternity, beyond time. Israel and Rome together struggled in historical time: an age with a beginning, a middle, and an end. That is the importance of the expanded range of historical topics found in the present Talmud. When, in the other Talmud, created in Babylonia, we find a still broader interest, in Iran as much as Rome, in the sequence of world empires past and present, we see how rich and encompassing a theory of historical events begins with a simple step toward a universal perspective. It was a step that I think, unlike the ancient prophets and apocalyptists, the scribes and priests represented by the Mishnah were incapable of taking.

The concept of periodization -- the raw material of historical thought -- hardly presents surprises, since apocalyptic writers began their work by differentiating one age from another. When the Mishnah includes a statement of the "periods" into which time is divided, however, it speaks only of stages of the cult: Shiloh, Nob, Jerusalem. One age is differentiated from the next not by reference to world-historical changes but only by the location of sacrifice and the eating of the victim. The rules governing each locale impose taxa upon otherwise undifferentiated time. So periodization constitutes a function of the larger system of sanctification through sacrifice. The contrast between "this world" and "the world to come," which is not a narrowly historical conception in the Mishnah, now finds a counterpart in the Talmud's contrast between "this age" and the age in which the Temple stood. And that distinction is very much an act of this-worldly historical differentiation. It not only yields apocalyptic speculation. It also generates sober and worldly reflection on the movement of events and the meaning of history in the prophetic-apocalyptic tradition. Accordingly, the Talmud of the Land of Israel presents both the expected amplification of the established concepts familiar from the Mishnah, and also a separate set of ideas, perhaps rooted in prior times but still autonomous of what the Mishnah in particular had encompassed.

Let us first survey what is new and striking. From the viewpoint of the Mishnah, as I have suggested, the single most unlikely development is interest in the history of a nation other than Israel. For the Mishnah views the world beyond the sacred Land as unclean, tainted in particular with corpse-uncleanness. Outside the holy lies the realm of death. The faces of that world are painted in the monotonous white of the grave. Only within the range of the sacred do things happen. There, events may be classified and arranged, all in relationship to the Temple and its cult. But, standing majestically unchanged by the vicissitudes of time, the cult rises above history. Now the ancient Israelite interest in the history of the great empires of the world -- perceived, to be sure, in relationship to the history of Israel -- reemerges within the framework of the documents that succeeded the Mishnah. Naturally, in the Land of Israel only one empire mattered. This is Rome, which, in the Yerushalmi, is viewed solely as the counterpart to

Israel. The world then consists of two nations: Israel, the weaker, Rome, the stronger. (This view varies somewhat from that of Leviticus Rabbah, seen in Chapter One.) Jews enjoy a sense of vastly enhanced importance when they contemplate such a world, containing as it does only two peoples that matter, of whom one is Israel. But from our perspective, the utility for the morale of the defeated people holds no interest. What strikes us is the evidence of the formation of a second and separate system of historical interpretation, beyond that of the Mishnah.

History and doctrine merge, with history made to yield doctrine. What is stunning is the perception of Rome as an autonomous actor, that is, as an entity with a point of origin, just as Israel has a point of origin, and a tradition of wisdom, just as Israel has such a tradition. These are the two points at which the large-scale conception of historical Israel finds a counterpart in the present literary composition. This sense of poised opposites, Israel and Rome, comes to expression in two ways.

First, as we shall now see, it is Israel's own history that calls into being its counterpoint, the anti-history of Rome. Without Israel, there would be no Rome -- a wonderful consolation to the defeated nation. For if Israel's sin created Rome's power, then Israel's repentance will bring Rome's downfall. Here is the way in which the Talmud presents the match (all translations are my own):

Y. Abodah Zarah 1:2

IV.   E.   <u>Saturnalia</u> means "hidden hatred" [<u>sinaah temunah</u>]: The Lord hates, takes vengeance, and punishes

F.   This is in accord with the following verse: "<u>Now Esau hated Jacob</u>" (Gen. 27:41).

G.   Said R. Isaac b. R. Eleazar, "In Rome they call it Esau's Saturnalia."

H.   <u>Kratesis</u>: It is the day on which the Romans seized power.

K.   Said R. Levi, "It is the day on which Solomon intermarried with the family of Phaorah Neccho, King of Egypt. On that day Michael came down and thrust a reed into the sea, and pulled up muddy alluvium, and this was turned into a huge pot, and this was the great city of Rome. On the day on which Jeroboam set up the two golden calves, Remus and Romulus came and built two huts in the city of Rome. On the day on which Elijah disapeared, a king was appointed in Rome: "<u>There was no king in Edom, a deputy was king</u>" (1 Kings 22:47).

The important point is that Solomon's sin provoked Heaven's founding of Rome, thus history, lived by Israel, and provoking anti-history, lived by Rome.

Quite naturally, the conception of history and anti-history will assign to the actors in the anti-history -- the Romans -- motives explicable in terms of history, that is, the history of Israel. The entire world and what happens in it enter into the framework of meaning established by Israel's Torah. So what the Romans do, their historical actions, can be explained in terms of Israel's conception of the world. A striking example of the tendency to explain Romans' deeds through Israel's logic is the reason given for Trojan's war against the Jews:

Y. Sukkah 5:1

VII.   A.   In the time of Tronianus, the evil one, a son was born to him on the ninth of Ab, and the Israelites were fasting.

      B.   His daughter died on Hanukkah, and the Israelites lit candles.

      C.   His wife sent a message to him, saying, "Instead of going out to conquer the barbarians, come and conquer the Jews, who have rebelled against you."

      D.   He thought that the trip would take ten days, but he arrived in five.

      E.   He came and found the Israelites occupied in study of the Light of Torah, with the following verse: "The Lord will bring a nation against you from afar, from the end of the earth, as swift as the eagle flies, a nation whose language you do not understand" (Deut. 28:49).

      F.   He said to them, "With what are you occupied?"

      G.   They said to him, "With thus-and-so."

      H.   He said to them, "That man [I] thought that it would take ten days to make the trip, but arrived in five days." His legions surrounded them and killed them.

      I.   He said to the women, "Obey my legions, and I shall not kill you."

      J.   They said to him, "What you did to the ones who have fallen do also to us who are yet standing."

      K.   He mingled their blood with the blood of their men, until the blood flowed into the ocean as far as Cyprus.

      L.   At that moment the horn of Israel was cut off, and it is not destined to return to its place until the son of David will come.

What is important here is the source of what we might call "historical explanation," deriving, as it does, from the larger framework of sages' conviction. Trajan had done nothing except with God's help and by God's design. Here is another example:

Y. Gittin 5:7

I.   A.   In the beginning the Romans decreed oppression against Judah, for they had a tradition in their hands from their forefathers that Judah had slain Esau, for it is written, "Your hand shall be on the neck of your enemies" (Gen. 49:8).

This means, again, that things make sense wholly in the categories of Torah. The world retains its logic, and Israel knows (and can manipulate) that logic.

At the foundations is the tension between Israel's God and pagan gods. That is, historical explanation here invokes the familiar polemic of Scripture. Accordingly, the development of an interest in Roman history -- of a willingness to take as important, events in the history of some nation other than Israel -- flows from an established (and rather wooden) notion of the world in which God and gods ("idols") compete. Israel's history of subjugation testifies, not to the weakness of Israel's God, but to his strength. The present prosperity of idolators, involving the subjugation of Israel, attests only to God's remarkable patience, God's love for the world he made. This conception, familiar to be sure in the Mishnah itself, now becomes absorbed into historical categories of "now" and "then." That is to say, the notion of competition between God and no-gods, Israel and Rome, is set within the framework of differentiation between (1) "this age" and (2) "the time to come." Since that notion marks a stop beyond the way in which the same theme had come to expression in Mishnah and Tosefta, we had best review the development of the same passage in its literary -- hence canonical -- sequences. The citation of (1) the Mishnah is underlined, the citation of (2) the subsequent Tosefta, in broken underline, followed by (3) the Yerushalmi's contribution in ordinary type.

Y. Abodah Zarah 4:7

A. They asked the sages in Rome, "If God is not in favor of idolatry why does he not wipe it out?"

B. They said to them, "If people worshiped something of which the world had no need, he certainly would wipe it out."

C. "But lo, people worship the sun, moon, stars, and planets.

D. "Now do you think he is going to wipe out his world because of idiots?"

E. They said to them, "If so, let them destroy something of which the world has no need, and leave something that the world needs!"

F. They said to them, "Then we should strengthen the hands of those who worship these, which would not be destroyed, for then they would say, 'Now you know full well that they are gods, for lo, they were not wiped out!'"

I. A. Philosophers asked the sages in Rome, "If God is not in favor of idolatry, why does he not wipe it out?" They said to them, "If people worshiped something of which the world had no need, he certainly would wipe it out. But lo, people worship the sun, moon, and stars. Now do you think he is going to wipe out his world because of idiots?" [M. 4:7A-D].

B. "But let the world be in accord with its accustomed way, and the idiots who behave ruinously will ultimately come and give a full account of themselves. If one has stolen seeds for planting, are they not ultimately going to sprout? If one has had sexual relations with a married woman, will she not ultimately give birth? But let the world follow its accustomed way, and the idiots who behave ruinously will ultimately come and give a full account of themselves" [T. A.Z. 6:7].

II. A. Said R. Zeira, "If it were written, 'Those who worship them are like them,' there would be a problem. Are those who worship the sun like the sun, those who worship the moon like the moon?! But this is what is written: 'Those who make them are like them; so are all who trust in them' (Ps. 115:8)."

B. Said R. Mana, "If it were written, 'Those who worship them are like them,' it would pose no problem whatsoever. For it also is written, 'Then the moon will be confounded, and the sun ashamed' (Is. 24:23)."

C. R. Nahman in the name of R. Mana, "Idolatry is destined in the end to come and spit in the face of those that worship idols, and it will bring them to shame and cause them to be nullified from the world."

D. Now what is the scriptural basis for that statement?

E.   "All the worshipers of images will be put to shame, who make their boast in worthless idols" (Ps. 97:7).

F.   R. Nahman in the name of R. Mana, "Idolatry is destined in time to come to bow down before the Holy One, blessed be He, and then be nullified from the world."

G.   What is the scriptural basis for that statement?

H.   "All worshipers of images will be put to shame...: all gods bow down before him" (Ps. 97:7).

The important point comes at II.C-H, at which the Talmud's sages present a temporal differentiation absent in the Mishnah. The problem of the Mishnah is a philosophical one. The Tosefta's anonymous authorities make that point explicit. There is a certain logic, an inevitability, upon which Israel may rely. True, idolatry prospers. But idolators will be called to account. Now that essentially atemporal notion, which can sustain the interpretation of a last judgment for individuals, moves into a social, hence temporal-historical, framework at the third stage. Not merely the idolator, as an individual, comes to account. The age of idolatry itself will come to an end. We differentiate between this age, which is bad, and another age, a period in time, which will be good. The notion of temporal sequences upon which historical thinking rests, in no way serves the framers of the Mishnah passage. By contrast, it is essential to the thought, concerning idolatry, of the authorities cited in the Talmud.

The concept of two histories, balanced opposite one another, comes to particular expression, with the Yerushalmi, in the balance of Israelite sage and Roman emperor. Just as Israel and Rome, God and no-gods, compete, with a fore-ordained conclusion, so do sage and emperor. In this age, it appears that the emperor has the power, as does Rome, as do the pagan gods with their temples in full glory. God's Temple, by contrast lies in ruins. But just as sages overcome the emperor through their inherent supernatural power, so too will Israel and Israel's God in the coming age control the course of events.

Y. Terumot 8:10
[Translated by Alan J. Avery-Peck]

IV.   A.   As to Diocles the swineherd, the students of R. Yudan, the Patriarch, would make fun of him.

B.   He [Diocletian] became emperor and moved to Paneas.

C.   He sent letters to the rabbis, [saying]: "You must be here [to see] me immediately after the end of the [coming] Sabbath."

D.   He instructed the messenger [who was to deliver these orders], "Do not give them the letters until the eve [of Sabbath], just as the sun is setting." [Diocletian hoped to force the rabbis to miss the appointment, for they would not travel on the Sabbath. Then he could have revenge on them because of their cavalier treatment of him, A.]

E.   The messenger came to them on the eve [of Sabbath] as the sun was setting.

F.   [After receiving the message] R. Yudan the Patriarch and R. Samuel bar Nahman were sitting in the public baths in Tiberias. Antigris, [a certain spirit, appeared and] came to their side.

G.   R. Yudan, the Patriarch, wished to rebuke him [and chase him away].

H.   R. Samuel bar Nahman said to him [Yudan], "Leave him be. He appears as a messenger of salvation."

I.   [Antigris] said to them, "What is troubling the rabbis?"

J.   They told him the story [and] he said to them, "[Finish] bathing [in honor of the Sabbath]. For your creator is going to perform miracles [for you]."

K.   At the end of the Sabbath [Antigris] took them and placed them [in Paneas].

L.   They told [the emperor], "Lo, the rabbis are outside!"

M.   He said, "They shall not see my face until they have bathed."

N.   [Diocletian] had the bath heated for seven days and nights, [so that the rabbis could not stand the heat].

O.   [To make it possible for them to enter, Antigris] went in before them and overpowered the heat.

P.   [Afterwards] they went and stood before [the king].

Q.   He said to them, "Is it because your creator performs miracles for you that you dispise the [Roman] Empire?"

R.   They said to him, "Diocles the swineherd did we despise. But Diocletian the emperor we do not despise."

S.   Diocletian said to them, "Even so, you should not rebuke [anyone], neither a young Róman, nor a young associate [of the rabbis, for you never know what greatness that individual will attain]."

The this-worldly and practical wisdom contained at the end should not blind us to the importance of the story within the larger theory of history presented in the Yerushalmi. The Mishnah finds ample place for debates between "philosophers" and rabbis. But in the Mishnah the high priest in the Temple and the king upon his throne do not weigh in the balance, or stand poised against, equal and opposite powers, the pagan priest in his temple, the Roman emperor on his throne. The very conception is inconceivable within the context of the Mishnah. For the Yerushalmi, by contrast, two stunning innovations appear: first, the notion of emperor and sage in mortal struggle; second, the idea of an age of idolatry and an age beyond idolatry. The world had to move into a new orbit indeed for Rome to enter into the historical context formerly defined wholly by what happened to Israel.

To our secular eyes these developments seem perfectly natural. After all, the Jews really had been conquered. Their Temple really had been destroyed. So why should they not have taken an interest in the history of the conqueror and tried to place into relationship with their own history the things that happened to him? We find self-evident, moreover, the comfort to be derived from the explanations consequent upon the inclusion of Roman history, in the Yerushalmi's doctrine of the world. But Israel had been defeated many times before the composition of the Mishnah, and the Temple had lain in ruins for nearly a century and a half when Judah the Patriarch promulgated the Mishnah as Israel's code of law. So the circumstances in which the Talmud's materials were composed hardly differed materially from the condition in which, from Bar Kokhba onward, sages selected from what was available and composed the Mishnah.

The Scriptures that, after all, also lay to hand offered testimony to the centrality of history as a sequence of meaningful events. To the message and uses of history as a source of teleology for an Israelite system, biblical writings amply testified. Prophecy and apocalyptic had long coped quite well with defeat and dislocation. Yet, in the Mishnah, Israel's deeds found no counterpart in Roman history, while, in the Palestinian Talmud, they did. In the Mishnah, time is differentiated entirely in other than national-historical categories. For, as in Abot, "this world" is when one is alive, "the world to come" is when a person dies. True, we find also "this world" and "the time of the Messiah." But detailed differentiation among the ages of "this world" or "this age" hardly generates problems in mishnaic thought. Indeed, no such differentiation appears. Accordingly, the developments briefly outlined up to this point constitute a significant shift in the course of intellectual events, to which the sources at hand -- the Mishnah, Tosefta, and Talmud of the Land of Israel -- amply testify.

Differentiation between the time in which the Temple stood and the present age, of course, hardly will have surprised the authors of the Mishnah. It was a natural outcome of the Mishnah's own division of ages. We recall how time was divided by the location of the altar, and how the divisions were explained by reference to what was done in that regard. Now we find a specification of the exact years involved. Not surprisingly, however, since the Mishnah does not speculate on when the Temple will be rebuilt, as in Tosefta, so here, the framers of the passage in Yerushalmi do not specify the year in which they think the Temple will be rebuilt. The Messiah's coming plays no role at all.

Y. Megillah 1:12

XI. O. So with the tent of meeting: it spent forty years less one in Gilgal. In Gilgal it spent fourteen years, seven when they were conquering the land and seven when they were dividing it.

P. In Shilo it spent three hundred and sixty-nine years.

Q. In Nob and Gibeon it spent fifty-seven years, thirteen in Nob and forty-four in Gibeon.

R. In Jerusalem in the time of the first building it was there for four hundred and ten years.

S. In the time of the second building it was four hundred ten years. This was meant to fulfill the statement of Scripture: "The latter splendor of this house shall be greater than the former, says the Lord of hosts; and in this place I will give prosperity, says the Lord of hosts" (Haggai 2:9).

Strikingly absent is any prediction as to when the third temple would be rebuilt. In due course many would take up the work of speculation and calculation. But, in his exegesis of the Mishnah, the author of this passage does not do so.

The principal point of differentiation between one age and another, now remained the destruction of the Temple, which, in the spirit of M. Sot. 9:15, marked the turn of the age. Rules held applicable to Temple times were reexamined to see whether they continued to apply. For example, "What is the law as to tearing one's garments at this time upon hearing God cursed in euphemisms?" (Y. San. 7:8 VII.C). But the important point is the least blatant. Not everything bad in the current age was to be blamed on the destruction. The explanation of contention in discussions of the law, for instance, involved not the differentiation between historical periods, but the (timeless) failure of the disciples. "In the beginning there was no contention; but ill-prepared disciples caused it" (Y. Hag. 2:1C). But the end of the matter still turns upon history: "The Torah is not going to be restored to its wholeness until the son of David comes (ibid., E).In context, the meaning is, "a long time from now." The step seems a small one. "This age" and "the other age" shifted at 70. Now, as soon as some other point of differentiation enters, not based upon the destruction of the Temple, a new possibility emerged. Specifically, the potentiality for a theory of Israel's life not spun out of the cult and its history begins to move toward realization. That much we can deduce from the slight evidence at hand.

A further mark of the development of interest in differentiating among historical periods is found in the commemoration of important events. Once one day is differentiated from another because of what happened on that same date a long time ago, we move away from the Mishnah's principal criterion for distinguishing the passage of time. How so? The framers of the Mishnah, following the priestly tradition, knew that one day differs from another because of the passage of the moon through fixed stars in heaven (e.g. Passover falls at the first full moon after the vernal equinox) and the consequent revision of the cultic offerings on earth (as at Numbers 28-29). True, as we noticed, sages also absorbed into their system one-time historical events, such as the seventeenth of Tammuz and the ninth of Ab. But those events proved incidental to the construction of a larger system, with Mishnah's tractates named for festivals of the natural year and focused upon Temple rites for those days. When, therefore, we discover units of discourse devoted to specific historical events and their meaning, we find outselves in a new situation. Why? Because events we regard as historical, as distinct from those we see as natural or supernatural, also have now come to be taken seriously. One day differs from another not by virtue of the criterion of creation, but on account of a political or other historical event. As we recognize, the only such historical, non-natural, event absorbed into the Mishnah's system involved the Temple. Accordingly, in what follows, we deal with a different approach to time from the one characteristic of the Mishnah's system.

Let me explain. Having evidently inherited from former times a calendar of celebrations of important events in Israel's history, marked by the prohibition against fasting, the Yerushalmi's sages pursued the issue. In the following unit of discourse we find attention to the traits of commemorative days, consonant with the interest in historical periodization noted earlier:

Y. Megillah 1:4

IX. B. On the twelfth of that month [of Adar] is Tirion's day. [That day on which the decrees of Trajan were annulled is a holiday and it is forbidden to fast on that day, contrary to Meir's view of acceptable behavior on the twelfth of Adar, in line with M. Meg. 1:4G.]

C. And R. Jacob bar Aha said, "Tirion's day has been annulled, for it is the day on which Lulianos and Pappos were killed."

D. The thirteenth of that month of Adar is Nicanor's Day.

E. What is Nicanor's Day? The ruler of the Kingdom of Greece was passing by the Land of Israel on route to Alexandria. He saw Jerusalem and broke out into cursing and execration, saying, "When I come back in peace, I shall break down that tower." The members of the Hasmonaean household went forth and did battle with his troops and killed them until they came to see those nearest the king. When they reached the troops nearest the king, they cut off the hand of the king and chopped off his head and stuck them on a pole, and wrote underneath them, "Here is the mouth that spoke shamefully and the hand that stretched out arrogantly." These he set up on a pike in sight of Jerusalem.

The importance of this passage is that attention focuses upon the meaning of days distinguished because of specific, one-time events that took place on them. There is no further taxonomic interest. The events are of a clearly historical character -- that is, in no way related to the cult or the natural course of the moon in the heavens -- and bear no claim that what happens matters only if the Temple is directly affected. True, in the background the Temple always is an issue. Further, the days under discussion appear on the so-called Fasting Scroll, on which it is forbidden to mourn; hence all the events fell into a single taxon. Yet the Mishnah's treatment of that matter neglects the very thing the Yerushalmi's authorities take up: the specifics of that happened, the exegesis, in its own terms, of the Scroll and the events to which it refers. And that is the main point. The framers of the passge at hand move out beyond the limits of the Mishnah's system when they narrate events essentially autonomous of happenings in the cult. Such events moreover are distinguished from one another and in no way forced into a uniform taxon. In this step, as in others we have reviewed, we see how the authors represented in the Yerushalmi move into a framework of thought in which Israel's being is described and interpreted in historical-eschatological terms, not in natural-supernatural ones.

Still, the Temple's destruction would always mark the caesura of time. Important political events were to be dated in relationship to that date. Israel lost the right to judge capital cases "forty years before the Temple was destroyed" (Y. San. 7:2III.A). So, too, forty years before the destruction, ominous signs of the coming end began to appear:

Y. Sotah 6:3

IV. A. Forty years before the destruction of the Temple the western light went out, the crimson thread remained crimson, and the lot for the Lord always came up in the left hand.

B.   They would close the gates of the Temple by night and get up in the morning
      and find them wide open.

C.   Said Rabban Yohanan ben Zakkai to the Temple, "O Temple, why do you
      frighten us? We know that you will end up destroyed.

D.   "For it has been said, 'Open your doors, O Lebanon, that the fire may devour
      your cedars!'" (Zech. 11:1).

Reference to the destruction of the Temple as a principal landmark in the division of
history, is hardly surprising. The framers of the Mishnah surely will not have been
surprised, since, for them, as M. Sot 9:15 shows, with the destruction, the old age had
turned into the new and darkening one. What was important to them was to find the
counterpart in the life of the sages, since the holy life of the Temple and the holy life of
the Torah-circles matched one another. So, in all, the Temple continued to provide the
principal, and generative, paradigm -- whether historical or cultic.

But as I have emphasized, the definition of significant, hence historical, events now
expanded to encompass things that happened beyond the Temple walls, yet still in
connection with the Temple's destruction. The main point is that, in the Talmud at hand,
the established symmetry was shattered. The Temple's destruction had been made the
counterpoise to the decline in the generations of sages. But now the Temple's destruction
stood for much more, testified, so to speak, in a wider variety of cases, then solely to the
decline of the supernatural world, whether priestly or scribal (to use our terms, not
theirs). The message of M. Sot. 9:15 was one thing, the message of the tales at hand, a
larger and more encompassing other story. That then is the turning point, the trans-
formation of the Temple's destruction into an event bearing consequences in many other
ways.

The most important change is the shift in historical thinking adumbrated in the
pages of the Yerushalmi, a shift from focus upon the Temple and its supernatural history
to close attention to the people, Israel, and its natural, this-worldly history. Once Israel,
holy Israel, had come to form the counterpart to the Temple and its supernatural life, that
other history -- Israel's -- would stand at the center of things. Accordingly, a new sort of
memorable event came to the fore in the Talmud of the Land of Israel. Let me give this
new history appropriate emphasis: It was the story of the suffering of Israel, the
remembrance of that suffering, on the one side, and the effort to explain events of that
tragic kind, on the other. So a composite "history" constructed out of the Yerushalmi's
units of discourse pertinent to consequential events would contain long chapters on what
happened to Israel, the Jewish people, and not only, or mainly, what had earlier occurred
in the Temple.

This expansion in the range of historical interest and theme forms the counterpart
to the emphasis, throughout the law, upon the enduring sanctity of Israel, the people,
which paralleled the sanctity of the Temple in its time. What is striking in the
Yerushalmi's materials on Israel's suffering is the sages' interest in finding a motive for
what the Romans had done. That motive derived specifically from the repertoire of
explanations already available in Israelite thought. In adducing scriptural reasons for the

Roman policy, as we saw, sages extended to the world at large that same principle of intelligibility, in terms of Israel's own Scripture and logic that, in the law itself, made everything sensible and reliable. So the labor of history-writing (or at least, telling stories about historical events) went together with the work of law-making. The whole formed a single exercise in explanation of things that had happened -- that is, historical explanation. True, one enterprise involved historical events, the other legal constructions. But the outcome was one and the same.

The components of the historical theory of Israel's sufferings were manifold. First and foremost, history taught moral lessons. Historical events entered into the construction of a teleology for the Yerushalmi's system of Judaism as a whole. What the law demanded reflected the consequences of wrongful action on the part of Israel. So, again, Israel's own deeds defined the events of history. Rome's role, like Assyria's and Babylonia's, depended upon Israel's provoking divine wrath, executed by the great empire. This mode of thought comes to simple expression in what follows.

Y. Erubin 3:9

IV.   B.   R. Ba, R. Hiyya in the name of R. Yohanan: "'Do not gaze at me because I am swarthy, because the sun has scorched me. My mother's sons were angry with me, they made me keeper of the vineyards; but, my own vineyard, I have not kept!' (Song 1:6). What made me guard the vineyards? It is because of not keeping my own vineyard.

      C.   "What made me keep two festival days in Syria? It is because I did not keep the proper festival day in the Holy Land.

      D.   "'I imagined that I would receive a reward for the two days, but I receive a reward only for one of them.

      E.   "'Who made it necessary that I should have to separate two pieces of dough-offering from grain grown in Syria? It is because I did not separate a single piece of dough-offering in the Land of Israel.'"

Israel had best learn the lesson of its history. When it did so, it also would take command of its own destiny. But this notion of framing one's own destiny should not be misunderstood. The framers of the Talmud of the Land of Israel were not telling the Jews to please God by doing commandments in order that they should thereby gain control of their own destiny.

To the contrary, the paradox of the Yerushalmi's system lies in the fact that Israel frees itself of control by other nations only by humbly agreeing to accept God's rule instead. The nations -- Rome, in the present instance -- rest in one pan of the balance, while God rests, as it were, in the other. Israel must then choose between them. There is no such thing, for Israel, as freedom from both God and the nations, total autonomy and independence. There is only a choice of masters, a ruler on earth or a ruler in Heaven.

With propositions such as these, the framers of the Mishnah will assuredly have concurred. And why not? For the fundamental affirmations of the Mishnah about the centrality of Israel's perfection in stasis -- sanctification -- readily prove congruent to the attitudes at hand. Once the Messiah's coming had become conditional upon Israel's condition, not upon Israel's actions in historical time, then the Mishnah's system will have imposed its fundamental and definitive character upon the Messiah-myth. An eschatological teleology framed through that myth then will prove wholly appropriate to the method of the larger system of the Mishnah.

What, after all, makes a Messiah a false Messiah? In this Talmud, it is not his claim to save Israel, but his claim to save Israel without the help of God. The meaning of the true Messiah is Israel's total submission, through the Messiah's gentle rule, to God's yoke and service. So God is not to be manipulated through Israel's humoring Heaven in rite and cult. The notion of keeping the commandments so as to please Heaven and get God to do what Israel wants -- such a nakedly manipulative system is totally incongruent to the text at hand. Keeping the commandments as a mark of submission, loyalty, humility before God -- it is this which marks the rabbinic system of salvation. So Israel does not "save itself." Israel never controls its own destiny, either on earth or in Heaven. The only choice is whether to cast one's fate into the hands of cruel, deceitful men, or to trust in the living God of mercy and love. We shall now see how this critical position is spelled out in the setting of discourse about the Messiah in the Talmud of the Land of Israel.

Bar Kokhba, above all, exemplifies arrogance against God. He lost the war because of that arrogance. In particular, he ignored the authority of sages:

Y. Taanit 4:5

X.   J.   Said R. Yohanan, "Upon orders of Caesar Hadrian, in Betar they killed eight hundred thousand."

K.   Said R. Yohanan, "There were eighty thousand pairs of trumpeteers surrounding Betar. Each one was in charge of a number of troops. Ben Kozeba was there, and he had two hundred thousand troops who, as a sign of loyalty, had cut off their little fingers.

L.   "Sages sent word to him, 'How long are you going to turn Israel into a maimed people?'

M.   "He said to them, 'How otherwise is it possible to test them?'

N.   "They replied to him, 'Whoever cannot uproot a cedar of Lebanon while riding on his horse will not be inscribed on your military rolls.'

O.   "So there were two hundred thousand who qualified in one way, and another two hundred thousand who qualified in another way."

P.   When he would go forth to battle, he would say, "Lord of the world! Do not help and do not hinder us! 'Hast thou not rejected us, O God? Thou dost not go forth, O God, with our armies'" (Ps. 60:10).

Q.   Three and a half years did Hadrian besiege Betar.

R.   R. Eleazar of Modiin would sit on sackcloth and ashes and pray every day, saying "Lord of the ages! Do not judge in accord with strict judgment this day!"

S.   Hadrian wanted to go to him. A Samaritan said to him, "Do not go to him, until I see what he is doing, and so hand over the city [of Betar] to you. ['Make peace... for you.']"

T. He got into the city through a drain pipe. He went and found R. Eleazar of Modiin standing and praying. He pretended to whisper something into his ear.

U. The townspeople saw [the Samaritan] do this and brought him to Ben Kozeba. They told him, "We saw this man having dealings with your friend."

V. [Bar Kokhba] said to him, "What did you say to him, and what did he say to you?"

W. He said to [the Samaritan], "If I tell you, then the king will kill me, and if I do not tell you, then you will kill me. It is better that the king kill me, and not you.

X. "[Eleazar] said to me, 'I should hand over my city.' ['I shall make peace...']."

Y. He turned to R. Eleazar of Modiin. He said to him, "What did this Samaritan say to you?"

Z. He replied, "Nothing."

AA. He said to him, "What did you say to him?"

BB. He said to him, "Nothing."

CC. [Ben Kozeba] gave [Eleazar] one good kick and killed him.

DD. Forthwith an echo came forth and proclaimed the following verse:

EE. "<u>Woe to my worthless shepherd, who deserts the flock! May the sword smite his arm and his right eye! Let his arm be wholly withered, his right eye utterly blinded!</u> (Zech. 11:17).

FF. "You have murdered R. Eleazar of Modiin, the right arm of all Israel, and their right eye. Therefore may the right arm of that man wither, may his right eye be utterly blinded!"

GG. Forthwith Betar was taken, and Ben Kozeba was killed.

We notice two complementary themes. First, Bar Kokhba treats Heaven with arrogance, asking God merely to keep out of the way. Second, he treats an especially revered sage with a parallel arrogance. The sage had the power to preserve Israel. Bar Kokhba destroyed Israel's one protection. The result was inevitable.

Now in noticing the remarkable polemic in the story, in favor of sages' rule over that of Israelite strong men, we should not lose sight of the importance of the tale for our present argument about the Messiah and history.

First, the passage quite simply demonstrates an interest in narrating events other than those involving the Temple, on the one side, or the sages in court, on the other. The story at hand and numerous others, not quoted here, testify to the emergence of a new category of history (or reemergence of an old one), namely, the history not of the supernatural cult, but of Israel the people. It indicates that, for the framers of those units of Yerushalmi which are not concerned with Mishnah-exegesis, and for the editors who selected materials for the final document, the history of Israel the people had now attained importance and demanded its rightful place. Once Israel's history thus reached center-stage, a rich heritage of historical thought would be invoked.

At that point, second, the Messiah, centerpiece of the history of salvation and hero of the tale, would emerge as a critical figure. The historical theory of the framers of the

Yerushalmi passage at hand is stated very simply. In their view Israel had to choose between wars, either the war fought by Bar Kokhba or the "war for Torah." "Why had they been punished? It was because of the weight of the war, for they had not wanted to engage in the struggles over the meaning of the Torah" (Y. Ta. 3:9XVI.I). Those struggles, ritual arguments about ritual matters, promised the one victory worth winning. Israel's history then would be written in terms of wars over the meaning of the Torah and the decision of the law.

True, the skins are new. But the wine is very old. For while we speak of sages and learning, the message is the familiar one. It is Israel's history that works out and expresses Israel's relationship with God. The critical dimension of Israel's life, therefore, is salvation, the definitive trait, movement in time from now to then. It follows that the paramount and organizing category is history and its lessons. As I suggested at the outset, in the Yerushalmi we witness, among the Mishnah's heirs, a striking reversion to biblical convictions about the centrality of history in the definition of Israel's reality. The heavy weight of prophecy, apocalyptic, and biblical historiography, with their emphasis upon salvation and on history as the indicator of Israel's salvation, stood against the Mishnah's quite separate thesis of what truly mattered. What, from their viewpoint, demanded description and analysis and required interpretation? It was the category of sanctification, for eternity. The true issue framed by history and apocalypse was how to move toward the foreordained end of salvation, how so to act in time as to reach salvation at the end of time. The Mishnah's teleology beyond time, its capacity to posit an eschatology lacking all place for a historical Messiah -- these take a position beyond the imagination of the entire antecedent sacred literature of Israel. Only one strand or stream, the priestly one, had ever take so extreme a position on the centrality of sanctification, the peripherality of salvation. Wisdom had stood in between, with its own concerns, drawing attention both to what happened and to what endured. But to wisdom what finally mattered was not nature or supernature, but rather abiding relationships in historical time.

This reversion by the authors of the Talmud to Scripture's paramount motifs, with Israel's history and destiny foremost among them, forms a complement to the Yerushalmi's principal judgment upon the Mishnah itself. For an important exegetical initiative of the Yerushalmi was to provide, for statements of the Mishnah, proof texts deriving from Scripture. Whereas the framers of the Mishnah did not think their statements required evidentiary support, the authors of the Talmud's Mishnah-exegetical units of discourse took proof-texts drawn from Scripture to be the prime necessity. Accordingly, at hand is yet another testimony to the effort, among third and fourth-century heirs of the Mishnah, to draw that document back within the orbit of Scripture, to "biblicize" what the Mishnah's authors had sent forth as a free-standing and "non-biblical" Torah.

The single most interesting indicator of the Talmud's framers' reversion to Scripture lies in the effort to go beyond systematizing biblical events and showing their taxonomic status. Now they proposed to draw lessons from biblical history. True, the framers of the Mishnah would not have been surprised at their heirs' effort to find in ancient Israel's writings lessons for the new day. They had done the same within the pages of the Mishnah itself. A glance, for example, at the homiletical materials at M. Ta. 2:1-4 shows how routinely they invoked biblical events, parallels, analogies. But the Mishnah contains no counterpart to vast stretches of the Yerushalmi's treatment of Scripture, specifically, its amplification of biblical stories with a view to rewriting the repertoire of history of ancient Israel. Evidence of that tendency will be found, for one example, in the rabbinization of the Messiah. So now a single if lengthy, example may suffice to make the point. Before us is a striking instance of the amplification of the narrative of a major event in ancient Israelite history.

Y. Abodah Zarah 1:1

I.   V.   Said R. Yudan, father of R. Mattenaiah, "The intention of a verse of Scripture [such as is cited below] was only to make mention of the evil traits of Israel.

      W.   "'On the day of our king when Jeroboam was made king the princes became sick with the heat of wine; he stretched out his hand with mockers' (Hosea 7:5).

      X.   "On the day on which Jeroboam began to reign over Israel, all Israel came to him at dusk, saying to him, 'Rise up and make an idol.'

      Y.   "He said to them, 'It is already dusk. I am partly drunk and partly sober, and the whole people is drunk. But if you want, go and come back in the morning.'

      Z.   "This is the meaning of the following Scripture, 'For like an oven, their hearts burn with intrigue; all night their anger smolders; in the morning it blazes like a flaming fire' (Hosea 7:6)."

      AA.   "'All night their anger smolders.'

      BB.   "'In the morning it blazes like a flaming fire.'

      CC.   "In the morning they came to him. Thus did he say to them, 'I know what you want. But I am afraid of your sanhedrin, lest it come and kill me.'"

      DD.   "They said to him, 'We shall kill them.'

      EE.   "That is the meaning of the following verse: 'All of them are hot as an oven. And they devour their rulers' (Hos. 7:7)...."

      KK.   When he would see an honorable man, he would set up against him two mockers, who would say to him, "Now what generation do you think is the most cherished of all generations?"

      LL.   He would answer them, "It was the generation of the wilderness which received the Torah."

      MM.   They would say to him, "Now did they themselves not worship an idol?"

      NN.   And he would answer them, "Now do you think that, because they were cherished, they were not punished for their deed?"

      OO.   And they would say to him, "Shut up! The king wants to do exactly the same thing. Not only so, but [the generation of the wilderness] only made one [calf], while [the king] wants to make two."

      PP.   [So the king took counsel and made two calves of gold] and he set up one in Bethel, and the other he put in Dan (1 Kings 12:29).

QQ. The arrogance of Jeroboam is what condemned him decisively.

RR. Said R. Yose bar Jacob, "It was at the conclusion of a sabbatical year that Jeroboam began to rule over Israel. That is the meaning of the following verse: '[And Moses commanded them]. At the end of every seven years, at the set time of the year of release, at the feast of booths, when all Israel comes to appear before the Lord your God at the place which he will choose, you shall read this law before all Israel in their hearing' (Deut. 31:10-11).

SS. "[Jeroboam] said, 'I shall be called upon to read [the Torah, as Scripture requires]. If I get up and read first, they will say to me, 'The king of the place [in which the gathering takes place, namely, Jerusalem] comes first.' And if I read second, it is disrespectful to me. And if I do not read at all, it is a humiliation for me. And, finally, if I let the people go up, they will abandon me and go over to the side of Rehoboam the son of Solomon.'

TT. "That is the meaning of the following verse of Scripture: '[And Jeroboam said in his heart, Now the kingdom will turn back to the house of David;] if this people go up to offer sacrifices in the house of the Lord at Jerusalem, then the heart of this people will turn again to their Lord, to Rehoboam, king of Judah, and they will kill me and return to Rehoboam, king of Judah' (1 Kings 12:27-28).

UU. "What then did he do? 'He made two calves of gold' (1 Kings 12:28), and he inscribed on their heart, '...lest they kill you' [as counsel to his successors].

VV. "He said, 'Let every king who succeeds me look upon them.'"

Familiar motifs, such as the danger of arrogance, occur here, just as in passages in which sages explain events of their own day. The main point, however, is not to be missed. The extensive recounting of biblical tales, the interest in making points through the narrative of historical events -- these do mark a break from the Mishnah's approach. For the framers of the Mishnah rarely found a use for the historical materials of Scripture. It is highly unusual to find in the Mishnah passages like this. Interest in expanding biblical history, apart from the salvific focus imposed by that history, testifies to the process at hand: the renewal, in the pages of the Yerushalmi, of the age-old practice of homiletical retelling of biblical tales. The earlier document contains slight signs of such interest; its successor is rich in such evidence.

The reversion to the prophetic notion of learning the lessons of history carried in its wake reengagement with the Messiah-myth. The climax of the matter comes in an explicit statement that the practice of conduct required by the Torah will bring about the coming of the Messiah. That explanation of the purpose of the holy way of life, focused now upon the end of time and the advent of the Messiah, must strike us as surprising in light of the facts surveyed in an earlier chapter.

For the framers of the Mishnah had found it possible to construct a complete and encompassing teleology for their system with scarcely a single word about the Messiah's coming when the system would be perfectly achieved. So with their interest in explaining events and accounting for history, third- and fourth-century sages represented in the units of discourse at hand invoked what their predecessors had at best found of peripheral consequence to their system. The following contains the most striking expression of the viewpoint at hand.

Y. Taanit 1:1

X.   J.   "The oracle concerning Dumah. One is calling to me from Seir, 'Watchman, what of the night? Watchman, what of the night?' (Is. 21:11)."

     K.   The Israelites said to Isaiah, "O our Rabbi, Isaiah, What will come for us out of this night?"

     L.   He said to them, "Wait for me, until I can present the question."

     M.   Once he had asked the question, he came back to them.

     N.   They said to him, "Watchman, what of the night? What did the Guardian of the ages tell you?"

     O.   He said to them, "The watchman says" 'Morning comes; and also the night. If you will inquire, inquire; come back again' (Is. 21:12)."

     P.   They said to him, "Also the night?"

     Q.   He said to them, "It is not what you are thinking. But there will be morning for the righteous, and night for the wicked, morning for Israel, and night for idolaters."

     R.   They said to him, "When?"

     S.   He said to them, "Whenever you want, He too wants [it to be] -- if you want it, he wants it."

     T.   They said to him, "What is standing in the way?"

     U.   He said to them, "Repentance: 'Come back again' (Is. 21:12)."

     V.   R. Aha in the name of R. Tanhum b. R. Hiyya, "If Israel repents for one day, forthwith the son of David will come.

     W.   "What is the Scriptural basis? 'O that today you would hearken to his voice!' (Ps. 95:7)."

     X.   Said R. Levi, "If Israel would keep a single Sabbath in the proper way, forthwith the son of David will come.

     Y.   "What is the Scriptural basis for this view? 'Moses said, Eat it today, for today is a sabbath to the Lord; today you will not find it in the field' (Ex. 16:25).

     Z.   "And it says, 'For thus said the Lord God, the Holy One of Israel, 'In returning and rest you shall be saved; in quietness and in trust shall be your strength.' And you would not' (Is. 30:15)."

The discussion of the power of repentance would hardly have surprised a Mishnah-sage. What is new is at V-Z, the explicit linkage of keeping the law with achieving the end of time and the coming of the Messiah. That motif stands separate from the notions of righteousness and repentance, which surely do not require it. So the condition of "all Israel," a social category in historical time comes under consideration, and not only the status of individual Israelites in life and in death. The latter had formed the arena for

Abot's account of the Mishnah's system's meaning. Now history as an operative category, drawing in its wake Israel as a social entity, comes once more on the scene. But, except for the Mishnah's sages, it had never left the stage.

We must not lose sight of the importance of this passage, with its emphasis on repentance, on the one side, and the power of Israel to reform itself, on the other. The Messiah will come any day that Israel makes it possible. If all Israel will keep a single Sabbath in the proper (rabbinic) way, the Messiah will come. If all Israel will repent for one day, the Messiah will come. "Whenever you want...," the Messiah will come. Now, two things are happening here. First, the system of religious observance, including study of Torah, is explicitly invoked as having salvific power. Second, the persistent hope of the people for the coming of the Messiah is linked to the system of rabbinic observance and belief. In this way, the austere program of the Mishnah, with no trace of a promise that the Messiah will come if and when the system is fully realized, finds a new development. A teleology lacking all eschatological dimension here gives way to an explicitly messianic statement that the purpose of the law is to attain Israel's salvation: "If you want it, God wants it too." The one thing Israel commands is its own heart; the power it yet exercises is the power to repent. These suffice. The entire history of humanity will respond to Israel's will, to what happens in Israel's heart and soul. And, with Temple in ruins, repentance can take place only within the heart and mind.

ii.   From Sanctification to Salvation

The framers of the Yerushalmi took over a document portraying a system centered upon sanctifying Israel through the creation of a world in stasis, wholly perfect within itself. They left behind them a document in which that original goal of sanctification in stasis competed with another. For within the pages of the Talmud of the Land of Israel we find a second theory of what matters in Israel's life. A system centered on the salvation of Israel in a world moving toward a goal, a world to be perfected only at the conclusion of the journey through time, now came to full expression. So the bridge formed by the Talmud of the Land of Israel leads from a world in which nothing happens but sanctification is, to one in which everything happens en route to salvation at the end.

To understand the choices at hand, let us revert to the points of contrast and tension, the specification of opposites, in the materials now reviewed. These indicate the range of permissible choices, hence the boundaries of the reality posited by a given universe of discourse. If we were to administer a psychological test to the storytellers, asking them to state the opposite of a given word, the results cannot be in doubt. If we say, "This world," the storytellers who speak of kings and wars would answer, "the world to come," or "this age," and "the age to come." If, by contrast, we presented to storytellers who relate tales of sages, a given symbol of the natural world, they would reply with a counterpart -- a symbol of the supernatural world. As we shall see in a moment, when (supernatural) rabbis die, for example, the (natural) world responds with miracles. In this sense, therefore, we confront two separate constructions of the world -- polar possibilities. The one involves historical-messianic explanation of historical events, the other, supernatural explanation of natural ones. True, prayer may speak of either kind of occurrence. But at the climactic moment on the Day of Atonement, the prayer of the high priest turned to the natural world:

Y. Yoma 5:2

II.   B.   This was the prayer of the high priest on the Day of Atonement, when he left the Holy Place whole and in one piece: "May it be pleasing before you, Lord, our God of our fathers, that [a decree of] exile not be issued against us, not this day or this year, but if a decree of exile should be issued against us, then let it be exile to a place of Torah.

       C.   "May it be pleasing before you, Lord, our God and God of our fathers, that a decree of want not be issued against us, not this day of this year, but if a decree of want should be issued against us, then let it be a want of [the performance of] religious duties.

       D.   "May it be pleasing before you, Lord, our God and God of our fathers, that this year be a year of cheap food, full bellies, good business; a year in which the earth forms clods, then is parched so as to form scabs, and then moistened with dew,

       E.   "so that your people, Israel, will not be in need of the help of one another.

       F.   "And do not heed the prayer of travelers [that it not rain]."

The high priest's prayer by itself obviously does not prove that, in all circumstances or contexts of sanctification, at issue are nature and supernature alone. But it does at least illustrate the self-evident association proposed at the outset. And the principal point must not be missed. One could speak of the ultimate resolution of Israel's present circumstance without invoking the name of the Messiah or the concept of events leading to a foreordained climax and conclusion with his coming at the end of time. Just as M. Sot. 9:15's author could refer to the resurrection of the dead with in the same breath speaking of the coming of the Messiah, so too it remained possible to do this in the pages of the Yerushalmi.

The main point is that for the framers of the Mishnah, one could speculate about the meaning and end of the holy way of life of the holy people without any reference to the coming of the Messiah. For them and their heirs in the Talmud of the Land of Israel the conception of redemption did not invariably invoke the salvific myth of the Messiah. Other units of discourse in the Yerushalmi carry forward this same treatment of the matter, as in the following.

Y. Yoma 3:2

III.   A.   One time R. Hiyya the Elder and R. Simeon b. Halapta were talking in the valley of Arabel at daybreak. They saw that the light of the morning star was breaking forth. Said R. Hiyya the Elder to R. Simeon b. Halapta, "Son of my master, this is what the redemption of Israel is like -- at first, little by little, but in the end it will go along and burst into light."

B.   "What is the Scriptural basis for this view? 'Rejoice not over me, O my
enemy; when I fall, I shall rise; when I sit in darkness, the Lord will be a light
to me' (Mich. 7:8)."

How then does the Judaism of sanctification, as represented in the Yerushalmi, take
up events we should regard as historical? That is, how is Israel to dispose of the events of
the day, if not through fervent prayer for the intervention of the Messiah? Bar Kokhba's
way, sages maintained, was arrogant. What alternative did they offer? The answer is
that, within the framework of sanctification, as in the Mishnah, so in the Yerushalmi,
world-shaking events were treated as trivial, with history converted into a symptom of
the condition of private life, and great events turned into epiphenomena within the
framework of everyday reality. Accordingly, within this system, as the Yerushalmi
expresses it, historical events play a decidedly subordinated role. Among the deeds that
do make history, mainly personal and private actions come to the fore, not those that bear
(to us) self-evident political and social consequence. Accordingly, historical events need
not take a leading role in the salvation of Israel -- even when salvation is at issue. The
"harsh decree" may be averted through piety, charity, right attitude -- surely not very
consequential deeds in the larger historical scheme of things.

Y. Taanit 2:1

IX.   A.   Said R. Eleazar, "Three acts nullify the harsh decree, and these are they:
prayer, charity, and repentance."

B.   And all three of them are to be derived from a single verse of Scripture:

C.   "If my people who are called by my name humble themselves, and pray and
seek my face, and turn from their wicked ways, then I will hear from heaven,
and will forgive their sin and heal their land" (2 Chron. 7:14).

D.   "Pray" -- this refers to prayer.

E.   "And seek my face" -- this refers to charity,

F.   as you say, "As for me, I shall behold thy face in righteousness; when I awake, I
shall be satisfied with beholding thy form" (Ps. 17:15).

G.   "And turn from their wicked ways" -- this refers to repentance.

H.   Now if they do these things, what is written concerning them?

I.   "Then I will hear from heaven and will forgive their sin and heal their land."

The forgiveness of sin draws in its wake prosperity, represented by the "healing of the
land." These references therefore cannot apply solely to what happens to the individual.
They deal with the fate of the whole of society. True, the harsh decree may come from
the state; but the outcome is the same. Through repentance and its associated actions
Israel can make its own history. In a statement like this, the issue of the coming of the
Messiah simply plays no role. The historical-salvific-messianic does not merge with the
timeless-sanctificatory-sagacious in materials of this kind; so far as I can see, within the
pages of the Yerushalmi, no such union appears.

In Israel there were holy men who bore within themselves the power to save Israel. In this framework, the notion of the Messiah loses all pertinence. How so? Every sage, if sufficiently holy, could effect miracles for Israel. Whether salvation is at issue remains in doubt. For, in context, we deal with supernatural, not this-worldly, events: a miracle in nature, effected by a holy man, rather than a one-for-all historical resolution of Israel's situation, that is, "salvation" in the ordinary sense. The power of the holy or righteous man to save Israel is made explicit in the following:

Y. Yoma 1:1

V.   D.   Said R. Hiyya bar Ba, "The sons of Aaron died on the first day of Nisan. And why is their death called to mind in connection with the Day of Atonement?

      E.   "It is to indicate to you that just as the Day of Atonement effects expiation for Israel, so the death of the righteous effects atonement for Israel."

      F.   Said R. Ba bar Binah, "Why did the Scripture place the story of the death of Miriam side by side with the story of the burning of the red cow?

      G.   "It is to teach you that, just as the dirt of the red cow [mixed with water] effects atonement for Israel, so the death of the righteous effects atonement for Israel."

The supernatural power associated with the death of the righteous person -- in this context, the sage -- appears in miracles marking the event.

Y. Abodah Zarah 3:1

II.   A.   When R. Aha died, a star appeared at noon.

      B.   When R. Hanan died, the statues bowed low.

      C.   When R. Yohanan died, the icons bowed down.

      D.   They said that [this was to indicate] there were no icons like him [so beautiful as Yohanan himself].

      E.   When R. Hanina of Bet Hauran died, the Sea of Tiberias split open.

      F.   They said that [this was to commemorate the miracle that took place] when he went up to intercalate the year, and the sea split open before him.

      G.   When R. Hoshaiah died, the palm of Tiberias fell down.

      H.   When R. Isaac b. Eliasheb died, seventy [infirm] thresholds of houses in Galilee were shaken down.

      I.   They said that [this was to commemorate the fact that] they [were shaky and] had depended on his merit [for the miracle that permitted them to continue to stand].

      J.   When R. Samuel bar R. Isaac died, cedars of the land of Israel were uprooted.

      K.   They said that [this was to take note of the fact that] he would take a branch [of a cedar] and [dance, so] praising a bride [at her wedding, and thereby giving happiness to the bride].

      L.   The rabbis would ridicule them [for lowering himself by doing so]. Said to them R. Zeira, "Leave him be. Does the old man not know what he is doing?"

M. When he died, a flame came forth from heaven and intervened between his bier and the congregation. For three hours there were voices and thunderings in the world: "Come and see what a spring of cedar has done for this old man!"

N. [Further] an echo came forth and said, "Woe that Samuel b. R. Isaac has died, the doer of merciful deeds."

O. When R. Yosa bar Halputa died, the gutters ran with blood in Laodicea.

P. They said [that the reason was] that he had given his life for the rite of circumcision.

The (natural) death of the sage invokes (supernatural) miracles, and so the sage enters into his eternal life. Not the Messiah alone, but any sufficiently holy and meritorious sage will mask in such a way the shift from one world to the next. But the worlds that are exchanged vary from system to system. For we do not find here the social history of Israel marked by the coming of the Messiah, but rather, the individual life of a sage commemorated in nature through supernature. The type of story at hand therefore calls into question the concept of one Messiah only, presiding over a unique event, at the end of a sequence of happenings all pointing toward that one-time eschatological climax. Either Israel is saved through the Messiah who resurrects the dead, or Israel is sanctified through the presence, in life and in death, of the righteous. We cannot demonstrate that these statements speak of different things to different people. We can only show, as I have here, that, when a unit of discourse deals with the one, it rarely, if ever, mentions the symbols or issues of the other.

But these sets of opposites -- time vs. eternity, life vs. death, nature vs. super-nature, on the one side, and history vs. end of time, this world vs. time of the Messiah, death vs. resurrection, on the other -- need not persist as separate and contradictory. The sage as holy man does his work now and does it mainly through ongoing nature and unchanging supernature. The Messiah -- as distinct from a (any) sage -- does his work at the end of time. He does it once. In the resurrection of the dead, he carries out a single, one-time action, by its nature one that need not be repeated. He is a single and therefore unique figure, a kind of holy man to be sure, but one of a kind, who performs a single, unique deed. Once a messiah, in the sense of a high priest appointed for a given task to be repeated many times, gives way to the Messiah, meaning, a man designed to do a single task, never to be repeated, we leave the framework of the Mishnah altogether.

This does not mean that people faced or even recognized a choice between one teleology and another. It means that the eschatology beyond history, the teleology beyond time, worked out in the Mishnah, stands essentially asymmetrical to the parallel theories spelled out here. They may be harmonized. They may set side by side without colliding. But they may not be represented as one and the same thing. They never meet. And, in the canonical literature of Judaism, the two theories of where things are heading scarcely intersect in a single pericope. The supernatural sage with his power over individual life and the natural world, and the eschatological Messiah with his command over the people of Israel and the whole of history -- both within the model of the rabbi, in the image of God -- never meet, except when King David is perceived as Rabbi David. And if truth be told, Rabbi David is mostly a rabbi, and only rarely a messiah or the Messiah. If we did not know that David was the prototype of the Messiah, the Yerushalmi would not have made us think so. In all, the eschatological messiah is difficult to locate. "Messiah" defines a category of holy man.

Chapter Six

TORAH AND ISRAEL'S NATIONAL SALVATION
IN THE TALMUD OF BABYLONIA

Judaism as we know it at the end of late antiquity reached its now-familiar definition when "the Torah" lost its capital letter and definite article and ultimately became "torah." What for nearly a millennium had been a particular scroll or book thus came to serve as a symbol of an entire system. When a rabbi spoke of torah, he no longer meant only a particular object, a scroll and its contents. Now he used the word to encompass a distinctive and well-defined world view and way of life. Torah now stood for something one does. Knowledge of the Torah promised not merely information about what people were supposed to do, but ultimate redemption or salvation. The shift in the use of the word, accomplished in a particular set of writings out of Judaism in late antiquity, appears dramatically in the following tale drawn from the last document to enter the canon, the Babylonian Talmud:

> R. Kahana [a disciple] went and hid under Rab's [his master's] bed. Hearing Rab "discoursing" and joking with his wife..., [Kahana] said to [Rab], "You would think that Abba's [Rab's] mouth had never before tasted the dish." [Rab] said to [Kahana], "Kahana, are you here? Get out! This is disgraceful!" [Kahana] replied, "My lord, it is a matter of torah, and I have the need to learn" (B. Ber. 62a).

As soon as we ask ourselves what the word, torah, means in such a context, we recognize the shift captured by the story. For -- to state the obvious -- to study "the Torah," meaning the Scriptures, one need not practice cultic voyeurism.

If, however, torah came to stand for something other than the particular writings comprising the ancient Israelite Scriptures, how do we trace the shift in content and usage? Clearly, the progress of the word and its meanings, both denotative and connotative, demands our attention. Within the expansion and revision of the word, originally referring to a set of books but in the end encompassing how one is to do even the most intimate deeds, we uncover the formative history of the Judaism for which the word Torah stands. That is the Judaism of the "one whole Torah," both written and oral, of "Moses, our rabbi" -- Judaism as it has flourished from late antiquity to our own day.

When we take up the issue at hand, therefore, we confront the symbol that stands for the kind of Judaism presented by the Talmuds and related literature, defined by the authority of the rabbis who stand behind those documents, and best described as "the way of Torah." So far as outsiders supply the name of a religion, the one at hand may be called "rabbinic Judaism," or "talmudic Judaism," for its principal authority-figure or authoritative document, or "normative Judaism," for the definitive theological status of the formulation at hand in the life of the Jewish people. But so far as insiders name the religion, that is, find language to capture and encompass the whole of what they do and believe, it is, as Kahana's statement tells us, "torah" -- "and I need to learn..."

The Torah of Moses clearly occupied a critical place in all systems of Judaism from the closure of the Torah-book, the Pentateuch, in the time of Ezra onward. But in late antiquity, for one group alone the book developed into an abstract and encompassing symbol, so that in the Judaism that took shape in the formative age, the first seven centuries A.D., everything was contained in that one thing. How so? When we speak of torah, in rabbinical literature of late antiquity, we no longer denote a particular book, on the one side, or the contents of such a book, on the other. Instead, we connote a broad range of clearly distinct categories of noun and verb, concrete fact and abstract relationship alike. "Torah" stands for a kind of human being. It connotes a social status and a sort of social group. It refers to a type of social relationship. It further denotes a legal status and differentiates among legal norms. As symbolic abstraction, the word encompasses things and persons, actions and status, points of social differentiation and legal and normative standing, as well as "revealed truth." In all, the main points of insistence of the whole of Israel's life and history come to full symbolic expression in that single word. If people wanted to explain how they would be saved, they would use the word Torah. If they wished to sort out their parlous relationships with gentiles, they would use the word Torah. Torah stood for salvation and accounted for Israel's this-worldly condition and the hope, for both individual and nation alike, of life in the world to come. For the kind of Judaism under discussion, therefore, the word Torah stood for everything. The Torah symbolized the whole, at once and entire. When, therefore, we wish to describe the unfolding of the definitive doctrine of Judaism in its formative period, the first exercise consists in paying close attention to the meanings imputed to a single word. In what follows, we deal with the final and climactic stage in the unfolding of meanings for the word Torah. We reach the Babylonian Talmud.

The Talmud of Babylonia marks the conclusion of the formation of the rabbinic canon in late antiquity. It is conventionally dated at about A.D. 500, though no evidence external to the document itself requires our placing a date on the document much before the ninth century A.D. By then, we find clear knowledge of the existence of the Babylonian Talmud, exhibited in writings wholly outside the framework of the Talmud itself. Sticking to established convention, however, we place the Talmud of Babylonia somewhere between A.D. 500 and 650.

The contents of the Talmud of Babylonia assuredly place the document at the end of the formative age. How so? Pretty much anything presented in the other documents we find in this one too. But what we find here we do not necessarily locate elsewhere, in compositions assumed to be of earlier date. The Talmud of Babylonia thus serves as a kind of summa and encyclopaedia of Torah -- that is, of Judaism. It contains almost everything we can demonstrate circulated earlier, while also preserving much else. The Talmud's modes of discourse are four: (1) exegesis of Mishnah and Tosefta, (2) abstract discourse on law in general, (3) exegesis of Scripture and (4) abstract discourse on mythic or theological themes of Scripture in general. So the Talmud of Babylonia joins together the available types of discourse on the Mishnah and on Scripture, making them into a single composition.

While both the national and the individual dimensions of salvation mark the measure of the word Torah in the Babylonian Talmud, the national proves the more interesting. For the notion of private salvation through "Torah" study and practice, of which we hear much, presents no surprise. When, by contrast, we find God saying, "If a man occupies himself with the study of the Torah, works of charity, and prays with the community, I account it to him as if he had redeemed me and my children from among the nations of the world" (B. Ber. 8a), we confront a concept beyond the imagination of the framers of Abot and the other compositions of that circle. Still more indicative of the importance for Israel as a whole, imputed to Torah-learning, is the view that those who master the Torah do not require protection by this-worldly means. Rabbis need not contribute to the upkeep of the walls of a town, "because rabbis do not require protection" (B. B.B. 8a). Sayings such as these focus to be sure upon the individual who has mastered the Torah. But the supernatural power associated with the Torah here is thought to protect not the individual alone, but Israelites in general associated with the individual Torah-master. So, given the social perspective of our sages, all Israel enjoys salvation through the Torah.

Of still greater interest, in the Talmud of Babylonia, study of the Torah takes the place of offering sacrifices in the Temple. Indeed, if a person studies the Torah, it is "as if" he has rebuilt the Temple:

B. Sanhedrin 99b
[Translated by H. Freedman, p. 675]

R. Alexandri said: He who studies the Torah for its own sake makes peace in the Upper Family and the Lower Family [men], as it is written, Or let him take hold of my strength [i.e., the Torah], that he may make peace with me; and he shall make peace with me (Is. 27:5). Rab said: It is as though he built the heavenly and the earthly Temples, as it is written, And I have put my words in thy mouth, and I have covered thee in the shadow of mine hand, that I may plant the heavens, and lay the foundations of the earth, and say unto Zion, Thou art my people (Is. 51:16). R. Johanan said: He also shields the whole world [from the consequences of its sins], for it is written, and I have covered [i.e., protected] thee in the shadow of mine hand. Levi said: He also hastens the redemption, as it is written, and say unto Zion, Thou art my people.

B. Sanhedrin 44b
[Translated by Jacob Shachter, p. 290]

R. Samuel b. Unia said in the name of Rab: The study of the Torah is more important than the offering of the daily whole offering.

The assertions in these pericopae take on more concrete meaning in light of yet another story. The house of Eli's iniquity "will not be expiated with sacrifice or offering for ever" (I Sam. 3:14), on which Rabbah said, "Not with sacrifice or offering but with words of the Torah" (B. Yeb. 105a). True, study of Torah by itself would never suffice; acts of lovingkindness also must accompany learning. But the striking comparison between sacrifice and study of Torah makes the main point. The study of Torah substitutes for the ancient cult and does for Israel now what sacrifice did then: reconcile Israel to its Father in heaven, wipe away sin, secure atonement, so save Israel. These deeply mythic convictions gave concrete expression to the view that the Torah not only sanctifies, but also saves, Israel. In the later history of Judaism, they became cliches. But once they were new and amazing claims, and this happened in the final stage of the formation of Judaism.

The dimensions of Torah-learning therefore no longer were bounded by the limits of the individual and his fate. Now they encompassed the life of Israel, the nation, and so spoke of the ongoing concern for the destroyed Temple and its cult. When, further, we consider that Temple and cult now formed central images in the expression of the messianic hope, with one important task of the Messiah conceived as the rebuilding of the Temple and the renewal of the sacrifices, the picture becomes fully clear. Through studying the Torah, the disciple took his place in the messianic process. His action bore the promise of rebuilding the Temple, that is to say, bringing the Messiah. His act of learning was to be compared to an act of sacrifice in the cult, that is to say, a foretaste of the messianic time to come. Accordingly, it required no great step from assertions such as these to the further conclusion that, as a symbol, the Torah bore within itself the entire teleological system of Judaism. Torah-study stood not only for things to be learned or done in the here and now. It pointed also -- even here and now -- toward the coming of the Messiah. So when we speak of the Torah as a source of salvation, we address very concrete and specific claims, hence expectations, and not merely generalized convictions about the worth of the rabbinic system as a whole.

Torah affords protection not only in time to come, but even now, a view expressed both in abstract terms, as we have seen, and also in concrete ones. Studying the teachings of the Torah deflects those who do so from paths leading to death to paths of life (B. Hag. 3b) and protects the disciple both in youth and in old age (B. Qid. 82b). These rather philosophical statements, however, do not reveal the practicality of the protection under discussion here. The following statements prove much more concrete:

B. Erubin 54a
[Translated by Israel W. Slotki, pp. 375-6]

R. Joshua b. Levi stated: If a man is on a journey and has no company let him occupy himself with the study of the Torah, since it is said in Scripture, For they shall be a chaplet of grace (Prov. 1:9).

If he feels pains in his head, let him engage in the study of the Torah, since it is said, For they shall be a chaplet of grace unto thy head.

If he feels pains in his throat let him engage in the study of the Torah, since it is said, And chains about thy neck.

If he feels pains in his bowels, let him engage in the study of the Torah, since it is said, It shall be a healing to thy navel (Prov. 3:8).

If he feels pain in his bones, let him engage in the study of the Torah, since it is said, And marrow to thy bones (Prov. 3:8).

If he feels pain in all his body, let him engage in the study of the Torah, since it is said, And healing to all his flesh (Prov. 4:22).

R. Judah son of R. Hiyya remarked: Come and see how the dispensation of mortals is not like that of the Holy One, blessed be He. In the dispensation of mortals, when a man administers a drug to a fellow it may be beneficial to one limb but injurious to another, but with the Holy One, blessed be He, it is not so. He gave a Torah to Israel and it is a drug of life for all his body, as it is said, And healing to all his flesh (Prov. 4:22).

B. Sotah 21a
[Translated by A. Cohen, p. 106]

The following did R. Menahem son of R. Jose expound: For the commandment is a lamp and Torah is light (Prov. 6:23) -- the verse identifies the commandment with a lamp and Torah with light; the commandment with a lamp to tell thee that as a lamp only protects temporarily, so [the fulfillment of] a commandment only protects temporarily; and Torah with light to tell thee that as light protects permanently, so Torah protects permanently; and it states, When thou walkest it shall lead thee (Prov. 6:22) -- "when thou walkest it shall lead thee," viz., in this world; "when thou sleepest it shall watch over thee," viz., in death; and when thou awakest it shall talk with thee, viz., in the Hereafter.

Parable of a man who is walking in the middle of the night and darkness, and is afraid of thorns, pits, thistles, wild beasts and robbers, and also does not know the road in which he is going. If a lighted torch is prepared for him, he is saved from thorns, pits and thistles; but he is still afraid of wild beasts and robbers, and does not know the road in which he is going. When, however, dawn breaks, he is saved from wild beasts and robbers, but still does not know the road in which he is going. When, however, he reaches the cross-roads, he is saved from everything.

The sayings just reviewed assign to the Torah a supernatural or magical power and treat its words as tantamount to prayers or incantations. The main point is that the kind of protection afforded by the Torah proves concrete and specific, immediate and practical. Study of Torah, after all, is as practical as offering an animal for sacrifice -- and bears equivalent consequences (B. Ber. 5a).

At the same time the Torah finds a place in the framework of psychological well-being. Specifically, the Torah serves as the antidote for sin: "If you occupy

yourselves with the Torah, you will not be delivered into the hand of the desire to do evil"
(B. Qid. 30b). The Torah serves, specifically, to control the impulse of human beings to do
what they should not. Indeed, the Torah was so shaped as to correspond in its teachings
to, and to forestall the impulses of humanity:

B. Shabbat 88b-89a
[Translated by H. Freedman, pp. 421-3]

R. Joshua b. Levi also said: When Moses ascended on high, the ministering angels
spake before the Holy One, blessed be He, "Sovereign of the Universe! What
business has one born of woman amongst us?" "He has come to receive the Torah,"
answered He to them. Said they to Him, "That secret treasure, which has been
hidden by Thee for nine hundred and seventy-four generations before the world was
created, Thou desirest to give to flesh and blood! What is man, that thou art
mindful of him, And the son of man, that thou visitest him? O Lord our God, How
excellent is thy name in all the earth! Who hast set thy glory [the Torah] upon the
Heavens!" (Ps. 8:5,2). "Return them an answer," bade the Holy One, blessed be He,
to Moses.

"Sovereign of the Universe" replied he, "I fear lest they consume me with the [fiery]
breath of their mouths."

"Hold on to the Throne of Glory," said He to him, "and return them an answer," as it
is said, He maketh him to hold on to the face of his throne, And spreadeth his cloud
over him (Job 26:9).

He [then] spake before Him: Sovereign of the Universe! The Torah which Thou
givest me, what is written therein? I am the Lord thy God, which brought thee out
of the Land of Egypt (Ex. 20:2).

Said he to them [the angels], "Did ye go down to Egypt; were ye enslaved to
Pharoah: why then should the Torah be yours?"

Again, What is written therein? Thou shalt have none other gods (Ex. 20:3): do ye
dwell among peoples that engage in idol worship?

Again what is written therein? Remember the Sabbath day, to keep it holy (Ex.
20:8): do ye then perform work, that ye need to rest?

Again what is written therein? Thou shalt not take [tissa] [the name... in vain] (Ex.
20:7): is there any business dealings among you?

Again what is written therein, Honour thy father and thy mother (Ex. 20:12); have ye
fathers and mothers?

Again what is written therein? Thou shalt not murder. Thou shalt not commit adultery. Thou shalt not steal; is there jealousy among you; is the Evil Tempter among you? Straightway they conceded [right] to the Holy One, blessed be He.

Immediately each one was moved to love [Moses] and transmitted something to him, for it is said, Thou hast ascended on high, thou hast taken spoils [the Torah]; Thou hast received gifts on account of man (Ps. 68:19): as a recompense for their calling thee man thou didst receive gifts.

The concrete salvation -- this-worldly benefit, other-worldly reward -- promised by the study of Torah set forth promises to be kept even now, and certainly in time to come. The shape of the program of rewards corresponds to the layout of sacrifices people made for Torah-study. If a disciple studied Torah in poverty, his prayer would be heard (B. Sot. 49a). If he studied when hungry so that his face became emaciated, in the world to come his face would shine. If he starved himself here, in the next world he would be satisfied (B. San. 100a). A person who meditated on the Torah only in appropriate places -- not in filthy alleys -- and who did so constantly could be expected to live a long time (B. Meg. 28a). When, therefore, the expectation that Torah-study would endow the disciple with supernatural power was disappointed, people wondered why:

B. Sanhedrin 106b
[Translated by H. Freedman, pp. 727-8]

Raba observed: Is there any greatness in propounding problems? In the years of Rab Judah the whole study was confined to Nezikin, whilst we study a great deal even of 'Ukzin, and when Rab Judah came to the law, "If a woman preserves vegetables in a pot" -- or as others say, "olives which were preserved with their leaves are clean," -- he observed, "I see here the discussion of Rab and Samuel;" whilst we, on the other hand, have studied 'Ukzin at thirteen sessions. Yet Rab Judah merely took off his shoes, and the rain came down, whilst we cry out [in supplication] but there is none to heed us. But it is because the Holy One, blessed be He, requires the heart, as it is written, But the Lord looketh on the heart (I Sam. 16:7).

The significance of this complaint that the latter generations know more Torah yet enjoy no supernatural power on that account is self-evident. People took for granted a correlation between mastery of Torah and supernatural power. Accordingly, Torah provided salvific power, both for the people Israel, and for the life of the individual and community.

Some solace for the disjuncture between mastery of Torah and the rewards of this life lay in the expectation of what awaited in Heaven. Specifically, Heaven presented a mirror of earth, the great below being small above. But those who were masters of Torah now would be great there too:

B. Pesahim 50a
[Translated by H. Freedman, p. 239]

R. Joseph the son of R. Joshua b. Levi, became ill and fell into a trance. When he recovered, his father asked him, "What did you see?"

"I saw a topsy-turvy world," he replied, "the upper [class] underneath and the lower on top."

He replied: "My son," he observed, "you saw a clear world. And how are we [situated] there?"

"Just as we are here, so are we there. And I heard them saying, 'Happy is he who comes hither with his learning in his hand.'"

Accordingly, the master of Torah, esteemed in this world, would be received in the world to come, even though others who are great in this world would come to nothing after death.

The stories and sayings cited at some length in some ways stand on a single continuum with the assertions of Abot. But they make claims that the framers of Abot never made. They express expectations for which in Abot we look in vain, even for the individual, of whom Abot does speak. In the Talmud the word Torah thus bears not only the entire range of established meanings, but an unanticipated and utterly fresh sense as well. This is in two ways.

First, Abot exhibits no counterpart to the concrete rewards for individual Torah-study laid out in the two Talmuds. What Abot promises is a rather general thing: encounter with the Presence of God. What the Talmuds propose to deliver contrasts in the specificity and concreteness of its character: power to make rain, healing of ailments, deliverance from material woes and for worldly, as well as other-worldly, life.

Second, I emphasize, the national and communal character of the salvation afforded in the two Talmuds' conception of the Torah seems to me to lack all precedent in the documents grouped around the Mishnah. The sage, for his part, serves not only himself, as in Abot, but the nation as a whole. The power enjoyed by the sage because of his knowledge of the Torah imparts benefit to the entire nation. It serves much as the cult and sacrifice once did. That, by definition, is service to the nation as a whole. I find no such stress in Abot upon the national dimension of the Torah's salvation.

Torah and Israel's National Salvation

The consequence of studying the Torah, moreover, bore important implications for the coming of the Messiah. So the doctrine of the study of Torah quite predictably fell into tandem with the teleology of the system as a whole. Yet we must ask how, in a very specific way, the doctrine accounted for the real, historical and social condition of the nation to whom it was addressed. What did the study of Torah have to do with the material, national context of Israel? To this last question, and the evidence of the Talmud of Babylonia concerning the answer, we now turn.

Before turning to the Babylonian Talmud, however, I have to specify the <u>type</u> of evidence under discussion. It consists of a single systematic and protracted essay upon the subject at hand, that is, an effort to spell out through a variety of completed pericopae a coherent position on the relationship of Israel to the Torah. Why does such a comprehensive construction seem to me by itself to be probative? The reason is that, when the Talmud of Babylonia presents essays on topics or themes independent of the Mishnah, these appear in some important cases to constitute what we might call encyclopaedia articles. That is to say, the framers of such essays assemble materials relevant to a given topic and work out a large statement of what they wish to say on that topic, through the selection and organization of pertinent sayings and stories. Quite separate from the Talmud's systematic constructions that elucidate and amplify a passage of the Mishnah and the legal principles contained therein, these autonomous essays prove more encompassing and may be deemed authoritative on doctrine.

For their topic, they also turn out to be unique. That is to say, a quick survey of protracted essays on various topics will yield only one systematic and protracted discussion of any given theme. Thus, on such a subject as honor due to mothers, resurrection of the dead, holiness of the Land, the person of Abraham, circumcision, the Messiah, and the like, we find one substantial aggregate of materials, and the aggregate will be unique in this Talmud. Individual or discrete materials assembled in such constructions may recur many times, to be sure. But as a redactionally whole and complete statement, the encyclopaedia-article on a stated theme (so far as I can see) does not. Why is this fact important?

It means that <u>the placement</u>, therefore, of such a systematic account of a topic, as much as the <u>contents</u>, reveals what the article's organizers deem striking about the topic. In the lengthy discussion of the Messiah (B. San. 99b-102a, cf. my <u>Messiah in Context</u>), for instance, the issue of the Messiah proved integral to the talmudic redactors' treatment of the Mishnah's chapter on individual Jews' enjoying a portion in the world to come. How so? Mention of the issue of the prevalent thesis of individual teleology -- life after death, the world to come -- provokes interest in the nation's collective teleology in eschatology. The two dimensions, individual and collective, serve to take the measure of the theme. While, in the end, the discussion of the Messiah in the context of the end of history alongside the individual in the context of death and resurrection yields no systematic account, the point is abundantly clear.

We come now to our topic, the Torah. So far as I am able to tell, we find on the theme of the Torah in the Talmud of Babylonia only one systematic and extensive composition -- that is, only one compilation of more than two or three autonomous pericopae. That composition runs on, as we shall now see, for many passages, constituting a lengthy and important statement on its own. The judgment of the framers of the composition on the meaning of the term Torah coincides with the position of the editors of the Talmud on where that discussion should be located. How so?

The point of the passage, in recurrent sayings, scriptural exegeses, and tales, is that the most important meaning of the word Torah lies in its defining who is Israel and who is not. The fate of the people Israel rests upon their faith in the Torah, their loyalty to the Torah.

And where do the Talmud's redactors choose to place the passage, but in the sole tractate of the Mishnah, hence of the two Talmuds, which addresses the relationship between Israel and the nations of the world?

By placing the composition at the head of Babylonian Talmud tractate Abodah Zarah, which deals with how Israel is to relate to gentiles on those occasions on which the gentile celebrates his pagan cult, the framers of the Talmud endorse the message of the compositors of the compilation. The individual sayings emphasize that Israel is Israel by virtue of the Torah. So the editors sort out Israel's relationships to the gentiles by reference to the Torah. The seventh-century Deuteronomists would hardly have been surprised: "For that will be your wisdom and your understanding in the sight of the peoples, who, when they hear all these statutes, will say, 'Surely this great nation is a wise and understanding people. For what great nation is there that has a god so near to it as the Lord our God is to us, whenever we call upon him? And what great nation is there, that has statutes and ordinances so righteous as all this Torah which I set before you this day?'" (Deut. 4:6-8). Whether the nations ever agreed (or even knew) is hardly at issue. What is important is the reaffirmation, at the end of the formation of Judaism, of the point at which it had all begun.

We turn now to the construction as a whole, abbreviated so as to omit extraneous material.

B. Abodah Zarah 2b-4a
[Translated by A. Mishcon, pp. 2-11]

I.   R. Hanina b. Papa (some say R. Simlai) expounded thus: In times to come, the Holy One, blessed be He, will take a scroll of the Torah in his embrace and proclaim: "Let him who has occupied himself herewith come and take his reward." Thereupon all the nations will crowd together in confusion, as it is said, "All the nations are gathered together" (Is. 43:9). The Holy One... will then say to them: "Come not before Me in confusion, but let each nation come in with its scribes...." Thereupon the Kingdom of Edom [Esau = Rome] will enter first before him. (Why first? Because they are most important....)

The Holy One, blessed be He, will then say to them: "Wherewith have you occupied yourselves?" They will reply: "O Lord of the Universe, we have established many market-places, we have erected many baths, we have accumulated much gold and silver, and all this we did only for the sake of Israel, that they might [have leisure] for occupying themselves with the study of the Torah."

The Holy One, blessed be He, will say in reply: "You foolish ones among peoples, all that which you have done, you have only done to satisfy your own desires. You have established market-places to place courtesans therein; baths, to revel in them; [as to the distribution of] silver and gold, that is mine, as it is written: Mine is the silver and Mine is the gold, saith the Lord of Hosts (Hag. 2:8); are there any among you who have been declaring this?" And "this" is nought else than the Torah, as it is said: _And_ this _is the_ Law <u>which Moses set before the children of Israel</u> (Deut. 4:44). They will then depart crushed in spirit.

On the departure of the Kingdom of Rome, Persia will step forth. (Why Persia next? -- Because they are next in importance.) The Holy One, blessed be He, will ask of them: "Wherewith have ye occupied yourselves?;" and they will reply "Sovereign of the Universe, we have built many bridges, we have captured many cities, we have waged many wars, and all this for the sake of Israel, that they might engage in the study of the Torah." Then the Holy One, blessed be He, will say to them: "You foolish ones among peoples, you have built bridges in order to extract toll, you have subdued cities, so as to impose forced labour; as to waging war, I am the Lord of battles, as it is said: <u>The Lord is a man of war</u> (Ex. 15:3); are there any amongst you who have been declaring <u>this</u>?" and "<u>this</u>" means nought else than the Torah, as it is said: _And_ this _is the_ Law <u>which Moses set before the children of Israel</u>. They, too, will then depart crushed in spirit. (But why should the Persians, having seen that the Romans achieved nought, step forward at all? -- They will say to themselves: "The Romans have destroyed the Temple, whereas we have built it.")

And so will every nation fare in turn. (But why should the other nations come forth, seeing that those who preceded them had achieved nought? -- They will say to themselves: The others have oppressed Israel, but we have not. And why are these [two] nations singled out as important, and not the others? -- Because their reign will last till the coming of the Messiah.)

The nations will then contend: "Lord of the Universe, hast Thou given us the Torah, and have we declined to accept it?"

(But how can they argue thus, seeing that it is written, <u>The Lord came from Sinai and rose from Seir unto them, He shined forth from mount Paran</u>? (Deut. 33:2). And it is also written, <u>God cometh from Teman</u> (Heb. 3:3). What did He seek in Seir, and what did He seek in Mount Paran? -- R. Yohanan says: This teaches us that the Holy One, blessed be He, offered the Torah to every nation and every tongue, but none accepted it, until He came to Israel who received it.

([How, then, can they say that the Torah was not offered to them?] Their contention will be this: "Did we accept it and fail to observe it?" But surely the obvious rejoinder to this their plea would be: "Then why did you not accept it?"

(-- This, then, will be their contention: "Lord of the Universe, didst Thou suspend the mountain over us like a vault as Thou hast done unto Israel and did we still decline to accept it?" For in commenting on the verse: <u>And they stood at the nether part of the mountain</u> (Ex. 19:17).

R. Dimi b. Hama said: This teaches us that the Holy One, blessed be He, suspended the mountain over Israel like a vault, and said unto them: "If ye accept the Torah, it will be well with you, but if not, there will ye find your grave.")

Thereupon the Holy One, blessed be He, will say to them: "Let us then consider the happenings of old... there are seven commandments which you did accept, did you observe them?"

The nations will then say, "Sovereign of the Universe, has Israel, who accepted the Torah, observed it?" The Holy One, blessed be He, will reply, "I can give evidence that they observed the Torah." "O Lord of the Universe," they will argue, "can a father give evidence in favor of his son? For it is written, Israel is My son, My firstborn" (Ex. 4:22). Then will the Holy One, blessed be He, say: "Heaven and Earth can bear witness that Israel has fulfilled the entire Torah." But they will [object], saying: "Lord of the Universe, Heaven and Earth are partial witnesses, for it is said, If not for My covenant with day and with night, I should not have appointed the ordinances of Heaven and Earth" (Jer. 33:25).

Then the Holy One, blessed be He, will say, "Some of yourselves shall testify that Israel observed the entire Torah. Let Nimrod come and testify that Abraham did not [consent to] worship idols; let Laban come and testify that Jacob could not be suspected of theft; let Potiphar's wife testify that Joseph was above suspicion of immorality; let Nebuchadnezzar come and testify that Hanania, Mishael and Azariah did not bow down to an image; let Darius come and testify that Daniel never neglected the [statutory] prayers; let Bildad the Shuhite, and Zophar the Naama-thite, and Eliphaz the Temanite [and Elihu the son of Barachel the Buzite] testify that Israel has observed the whole Torah."

The nations will then plead, "Offer us the Torah anew and we shall obey it." But the Holy One, blessed be He, will say to them, "You foolish ones among peoples, he who took trouble [to prepare] on the eve of the Sabbath can eat on the Sabbath, but he who has not troubled on the eve of the Sabbath, what shall he eat on the Sabbath? Nevertheless, I have an easy command which is called Sukkah; go and carry it out."

Straightaway will every one of them betake himself and go and make a booth on the top of his roof; but the Holy One, blessed be He, will cause the sun to blaze forth over them as at the Summer Solstice, and every one of them will trample down his booth and go away, as it is said, Let us break their bands asunder, and cast away their cords from us.

Thereupon the Holy One, blessed be He, will laugh at them, as it is said, He that sitteth in heaven laugheth (Ps. 2:4).

II.   Rab Judah said in the name of Rab: "The day consists of twelve hours; during the
        first three hours the Holy One, blessed be He, is occupying Himself with the Torah,
        during the second three He sits in judgment on the whole world, and when He sees
        that the world is so guilty as to deserve destruction, He transfers Himself from the
        seat of Justice to the seat of Mercy; during the third quarter, He is feeding the
        whole world, from the horned buffalo to the brood of vermin; during the fourth
        quarter He is sporting with the leviathan....

III.   R. Levi says: He who discontinues [learning] words of the Torah and indulges in idle
        gossip will be made to eat glowing coals of juniper, as it is said, They pluck
        salt-wort with wormwood; and the roots of juniper are their food (Job 30:4).

IV.   Resh Lakish says: To him who is engaged in the study of the Torah by night, the
        Holy One extends a thread of grace by day, as it is said, By day the Lord will
        command his lovingkindness, and in the night his song shall be with me (Ps. 42:9).

V.   Rab Judah says in the name of Samuel: Why is it written, And Thou makest man as
        the fishes of the sea, and as the creeping things, that have no ruler over them (Hab.
        1:14)? Why is man here compared to the fishes of the sea? To tell you, just as the
        fishes of the sea, as soon as they come on to dry land, die, so also man, as soon as he
        abandons the Torah and the precepts [incurs destruction].

What is important in the present composite is the lengthy opening narrative (I). It speaks
neither of the study of Torah, on the one side, nor of the keeping of the teachings of the
Torah, on the other. Here the scroll of the Torah -- imagined in total abstraction! --
serves to distinguish between Israel and the empires, Rome, Persia, then all other nations,
and to explain why Israel alone enjoys God's favor. "Torah" is the reason, meaning
studying and keeping the Torah, or, in modern language, practicing "Judaism." In the
story-teller's vision, the nations seek justification before God by appealing to how they
have served the Torah through service to Israel. The humor and irony can scarcely be
missed, since God's replies, through the unfolding of the tale, make them explicit. Then
the nations exculpate themselves by saying that, after all, God never gave them the Torah
anyhow. The story proceeds (in what seems to me a zigzag) to demonstrate that, in any
event, Israel did keep the Torah. Gentile witnesses, Laban, Potiphar's wife, Nebuchadnezzar, Darius, and the like, all testify that Israel really did observe the whole Torah.
The nations then ask for a chance to keep the Torah and are given it -- with disastrous
results. The story joins the two principal meanings associated with the Torah, studying it
and carrying out its commandments, and in the aggregate makes a fresh and startling
point. It is, as I said, that Israel is justified because it has kept and has studied the
Torah, This bears obvious implications for what Israel must continue to do. A story such
as this shows how the word Torah stands for the doctrine of Judaism.

        The remainder of the composite presents no surprises. God spends a fourth of the
day studying Torah (II). One who stops learning words of Torah and uses his tongue for

gossip will be burned (III). Studying Torah by night, when people usually sleep, is especially meritorious and provokes a good reward (IV). When a person abandons the Torah and commandments, destruction follows (V). All of these are conventional; the purpose in including them, it seems to me, is simply to ring the changes on familiar assertions. They serve to turn the whole into a composite, so the long story becomes something more, as I said at the outset. Now, finally, we have a complete picture of what people call to mind when they speak of the word Torah.

Once the Torah serves to explain the condition of Israel among the nations, we move from the realm of other-worldly discourse about encounter through the Torah with God, to the immediate society of flesh-and-blood mortals. For in this last rubric we find how the Torah as an abstract symbol is made to serve the concrete interests of the people Israel, in its this-worldly historical life, its politics, its ongoing national experience. Israel emerged from the formative centuries at hand to live in a single way under diverse circumstances, to shape its life in accordance with the way of Torah. From England in the far north and west to India and even remote China, Jews lived in accordance with the religious system at hand and found it self-evident that the system made sense. So they explained to themselves who they were, and who the nations were, by invoking the message of the Torah, much as the story at hand portrayed that message. Judaism, in its final symbolic formulation in the era now closing in the last pages of the Babylonian Talmud, told the people Israel who it was and why it lived where and how it did, who the nations were, and why they treated Israel the way they did (the only thing important, after all, about the nations).

So as uniform symbol of many diverse things, the Torah served to state the substance of the message in every possible medium -- material and intellectual, as concrete object, in human form, and as abstract arbiter of matters of status, social and personal. The symbol of the Torah served to classify things on earth and (in the minds of the faithful) in Heaven as well. For the succeeding centuries, until nearly our own day, time stood still and life remained the same for Israel under the aspect of the Torah. When we ask for other eternal components of late antiquity's legacy to the West, we find the Torah standing not quite alone, to be sure, but not on a crowded stage: on a dark stage pinpointed in a shaft of light along with philosophy, Christianity, Islam, and law -- but not much more.

Part Three

CONTEMPORARY AFTERWORD

Chapter Seven

TORAH TODAY:
LERNEN AND LEARNING IN SAMUEL C. HEILMAN'S PEOPLE OF THE BOOK

If, as I have argued in the preceding chapter, the symbol of Torah serves to express the message of Israel's life as a nation, then the disposition of that symbol in modern and contemporary times will bear rich meaning. Specifically, it will speak, far beyond its own limits, about the condition of Israel, the Jewish people, in relationship to its inherited and established symbols of socialization. Since for a millenium and a half, the Torah served as the principal symbol of Israel's social life, its sanctification and salvation, and study of the Torah defined the critical act in realization of that symbol, the status of the symbol proves suggestive. Just as social change testifies to symbol change -- the burden of the first six chapters of this book -- so symbol change is apt to tell us something about social change. In what follows, I focus upon a recent and authoritative account of how the Torah is studied as an avocation by Jews who, in doing so, deem themselves to be pious. I draw the contrast between the substance of the symbol -- Torah-learning -- and the manner in which the symbol reaches social reality -- Torah-study in synagogue and yeshiva alike by amateurs. The symbol over the centuries had gained weighty and dense intellectual substance. Today the same symbol turns out to be invoked to stand for an activity of slight intellectual substance. Study of Torah turns out to constitute a ritual of little study and virtually no torah. What that fact about the contemporary status of the ancient symbol suggests beyond itself I cannot say. While, as I said, symbol change is social change, the fact that the Jews exhibit symptoms of fundamental social change brings no news.

Everybody knows that the Jews are the people of the Book, as Muhammed called them, but also the people whose religious life centers around the study of holy books. It is a commonplace that, through the work of studying those books, people express their piety and seek to attain holiness. Now that cannot be regarded as "pretty much how things are," for, we know, in other religious traditions piety comes about in other ways, for example, through a life of poverty and service to the poor, or through heroism in the battlefield in the service of the faith, or through holy vagrancy, celibacy, saying prayers, and so on through a very long list. It is distinctive to Judaism that, when you study certain books you are changed, made holy.

The word in Yiddish is lernen, and it means a spiritual meditation on Jewish books of a certain character. Some "learned" full-time, and many did some of the time. Now the important fact is that we deal, in lernen, or in Talmud Torah, with something more than the mere acquisition of facts. If people think that when Jews express piety through study of the Torah, they come for information only or mainly, they truly misconstrue what is at issue.

In a brilliant work of ethnography, Samuel Heilman (The People of the Book. Drama, Fellowship, and Religion [Chicago, 1983: The University of Chicago Press]) tells how he set out to write a book about Jews who study Torah, or "learn," as an avocation. (He does not treat those who do it all the time.) He noticed the fact to which I just now alluded, namely, at issue was not merely the acquisition of knowledge, but something else. In that connection he makes an important observation (p. 2):

> From early on I realized that, for many of the Jews I was observing, this experience was more than simply the assimilation of knowledge. For one thing, many of those I watched had been lernen for years, but still seemed to be unable to review the texts on their own or recall very much of the content in front of them. For another, even those who had lernt a lot and displayed an erudite familiarity with the texts took apparent great pleasure in repeating what they had already studied rather than looking for the new and as yet unknown. The best lernen, it seemed, was the sort which reiterated what everyone already knew. The best questions to ask were those the texts themselves asked; and the best if not the only true answers were those already written on the pages open before one. Finally, while the members of the study circles I observed ostensibly gathered in the house of study to get the wisdom of Judaism from the books into their minds, they often spent more time in class getting their feelings about Judaims off their chests. Clearly much more than learning or the accumulation of information about Jewish texts was going on. I wanted to find out what that something more was [italics supplied].

Heilman's reflections on what he saw in many years of observing the process of study of Torah, or lernen, present us with a puzzle. We take for granted that we learn in order to know things; we know in order to understand things. Learning is a process of problem-solving. It helps us to understand, to appreciate. When we learn, we grow, we change, we live our lives in a greater framework of comprehension, in a larger dimension of meaning.

That description of what I believe people do when they learn things omits reference to the one dimension important in Talmud Torah or lernen. When we study arithmetic, or even ethics, we do not claim to become holy men and women. We become better informed; we may even improve our intellectual powers; we might even turn out to be happier or possibly better human beings. But the dimension of holiness measures nothing, defines nothing, affects nothing. And, for the processes of Talmud Torah or lernen, the ultimate goal is sanctification. What is learned may appear to be secular facts. But the source of what is learned, which is Torah, and the intent of the ones who do the learning, which is to study Torah, reshape the intellectual act into a religious quest, a holy event.

Now when Heilman therefore states that among hobbyists he observed "more than simply the assimilation of knowledge," he points toward what distinguishes the act of study of Torah from all other acts of learning, the setting of the study-house and circle of rabbi and disciples from all other situations of intellect, and the process of teaching and studying Torah from all other processes by which people enlarge their intellects and enhance their knowledge. And yet, the act remains the same, the use of the mind, the formation of a social group for the acquisition of knowledge and -- it is always a social group -- the improvement of one's status. So how different is this act of learning that is different from all other acts of learning, this Talmud Torah, this realm of lernen? The verbal explanation invokes language and image not routinely associated with schooling and study. But the act itself -- use of the mind -- remains what it is. Whether you use your power of understanding to study history or Jewish law, to master mathematics or the traditional interpretation of the Hebrew Scriptures, the power that you use remains what it is.

If that is the case, then we must find astonishing Heilman's characterization of this "experience" that is "more than simply the assimilation of knowledge." Heilman makes three points:

1.   The students after many years do not learn very much: "unable to review the texts on their own or recall very much of the content in front of them." My own observations of students who return to my university -- and they were not hobbyists -- after a year of study in an Israeli yeshiva correspond to Heilman's. When I ask them what they learned, they name the tractate. When I ask them the main point of the tractate, or of the part of it they supposedly learned, they are dumbfounded. They never learned. Unlike university learning, their process of study involved reading little or nothing on their own, writing nothing on their own, pursuing no questions beyond those raised and answered in the class room. And the class in Torah-study, as I am able to investigate its properties, consists of a river of words, flowing out of the mouth of the rabbi, scarcely eddying up to the shores, into the overstuffed ears of the disciple. Learning which does not equip the students to do on their own what the teacher teaches yields not education but "something else."

2.   The students enjoy repeating what they know. The process is one of rehearsing the message, saying in intricately subtle ways what everyone knows, reaffirming the given. So learning forms a labor not of discovery and testing, but of repetition and revalidation. Then the relationship of teacher to student finds definition in the authority of the one, the subordination of the other, the affirmation of the teacher's authority by the student, the reassurance of the student by the teacher. Learning becomes a process not of discovery but of renewal, not of inquiry and the testing of possibilities but of displaying, in intellectual form, one's loyalty and devotion to the revealed truths of the faith. So, as Heilman says, the students took "great pleasure in repeating what they had already studied rather than looking for the new and as yet unknown. The best lernen... was the sort which reiterated what everyone already knew." So you ask only when you know the answer, and the purpose of asking is to hear the reassuring and familiar answer.

3. A great deal of class time is spent in free-associating, expressing how people feel, chatting about this and that -- all under the auspices of God and revealed Torah. Heilman says that among the hobbyists whom he studied "much more than learning... was going on." But his book demonstrates that a great deal less than learning also was going on: experience, not intellect; emotion, not disciplined speculation and imagination; transactions of a private and individual character, not a public exchange of reasoned and well-constructed argument. If people come to class to get "their feelings about Judaism off their chests," then they do not come to learn at all. For the one thing you do not do when you tell people how you feel is learning something about the world beyond yourself.

Now Heilman must face the charge of misinterpreting what he saw. But I doubt anyone can make the charge stick. For he details what he observed over many years, in many settings of avocational lernen, and, in my more limited experience, the anecdotes he reports, the generalizations he draws, the picture he composes -- these do indeed capture the reality of lernen or Talmud Torah in our day. Perhaps in some remote or isolated place a quite different transaction takes place when people as a hobby or avocation open the holy books of Judaism with that same intent that brings them to do so in yeshivas and related settings, namely, to attain sanctification. But in the main, lernen is ritual-learning. And ritual learning has nothing to do with the two things we in the secular West associate with the intellect: learning and attaining understanding.

To state matters simply: lernen and learning have little to do with one another. We teachers aim through teaching to make ourselves obsolete. We want our students to be able to do things on their own. If my students after many years could not review texts on their own or remember the content before them, I should regard my teaching as worthless. If my students could only repeat what I say, without critical examination and renewal, I should regard my teaching as hopeless. If my classroom were a place in which people mainly free-associated about whatever they had on their minds, a place with no program and no purpose, I should regard my teaching as pointless. So far as Heilman's characterization of the something more -- and the something less -- of Talmud Torah or lernen as he saw it proves accurate, therefore, I have to judge the so-called "traditional" setting for Jewish learning as worthless, hopeless, and pointless.

Does Jewish learning in a secular context exhibit worth, hope, a point? What difference does it make if, as in the academy, the labor points not toward the sanctification of the student, the rehearsal of the kerygma of the faith, the validation and reaffirmation of "the tradition," but toward discovery and renewal of interest and insight? To these questions we have now to turn. For the task of public discourse of intellect is not to celebrate but to analyze. Were I merely to propose a new intellectual orthodoxy to take the place of a discredited and decayed old one, I should serve no lasting end. Indeed, it is not my purpose merely to add to the injuries already inflicted upon the tradition of Jewish learning by the practitioners of lernen. What I wish to propose is that lernen as Heilman describes it bears no true witness to lernen as the great masters of Talmud Torah have practiced it in the past, and, in some few instances, vocational students practice it today as well.

Let me then propose two propositions.

First, the one just now introduced: lernen as Heilman portrays it and Talmud Torah as the classsic texts of Judaism portray it bear slight resemblance to one another.

Second, the sources for the renewal of a truly intellectual encounter with Jewish tradition flow from those same attitudes of mind that we today cultivate in the secular academy: criticism, freedom of imagination and inquiry, devotion to learning as a process of enlightenment, a quest for understanding.

Anyone who opens the classical texts of Judaism, from the Mishnah onward through the two Talmuds, the various compositions organized around the exegesis of Scripture, the speculative works of philosophers and mystics, the constructive works of legal codifiers and social philosophers of Judaism, onward through the remarkably original creations of modern times in Hasidism, in Hebrew literature, in modern Jewish thought and learning -- anyone familiar with even a book, even a chapter, even a sentence, of that vast corpus must assent to one claim. When we study Torah, we are meant to encounter matters of intellect, ideas, problems of inquiry. Study of Torah begins (though it does not and should not end) with the use of our minds. When, moreover, we do use our minds, it is to learn. No authentic master of the Torah in its 3500 years of unfolding can agree that study of Torah characterizes the accomplishment of people who cannot review on their own or remember much of what they are supposed to have learned. Ritual learning has nothing to do with study of Torah, even though, in sizable circles, studying Torah constitutes little more than an empty ritual.

Second, study of Torah assuredly requires us to repeat and even to memorize. There is no learning without acquisition of facts, of texts and their contents, accurately interpreted. The opposite of learning is making things up as we go along. That we cannot do if we wish to stand within the rigorous tradition of Talmud Torah. But when you study Talmud, you reason. When you take up the commentaries to the written Torah, you must try to understand the questions they ask, the answers they offer. Learning requires more than rehearsing the message, repeating what we hear like dumbbells. Learning means understanding, and understanding transcends mere repetition of what others have explained, repeating holy words like incantations. True, not everyone can attain a high level of reasoning, of critical inquiry. But few are so ungifted that they cannot do more than repeat, without true comprehension, two and two are four, or "In the beginning God created the world" or "When do people recite the Shema in the evening?" The notion that, when we learn, what we mainly do is define a relationship to an authority figure, moreover, contradicts the purpose of learning defined in every text of Judaism. That purpose is simple. We learn in order to carry out what we learn, not merely to replicate the teacher. It goes without saying that in order to do something intelligently and sincerely, we have not merely to assent to, but also to understand, the truth at hand. Anything else means merely to go through the motions. Talmud Torah is meant to create greater, more holy human beings, not oxen and dumb asses.

Third, all of the texts of Judaism, early and late, exhibit the single trait of careful organization, deeply reflective purpose. Talmud Torah brings us to texts that always make a point, always follow a program, always seek to impart meaning. True, that meaning, the order and purpose, may not always rise to the surface. But no text of Judaism is mere gibberish. None involves only free association. The two Talmuds sometimes are misrepresented as formless and aimless, a mere mass of this-and-that. But people who so represent the Talmuds have not carefully inquired into the reasons that their materials follow the order that they do, rather than some other order or no order at all. Everyone who has covered the whole of a tractate can explain the order of that tractate. Anyone familiar with more than a few lines, chosen haphazardly, recognizes that principles of form and logic govern the layout of the literature. So when people think that Talmud Torah permits or even requires free association, they misconstrue the substance and the form, the aesthetics and the logic, of Torah. True enough, Talmud Torah speaks to our hearts and not only to our minds. When we study Torah we gain not only information but also experience. We feel as well as think, experience emotion as well as gain insight. But all of this rightly done responds to the plan and the order of our texts: we feel the things the founders and dreamers of our texts want us to feel, our hearts respond to the heart-felt plea of the words the authors of our texts so cast that we would respond in our hearts. Indeed, when we study Torah without committing the heart, the imagination, the emotion, we gain mere information, and little enough of that.

But the right route to the heart of the Torah leads outward _from_ the Torah. Our learning requires us to bring the teachings of the Torah to our context. We carry the text outward to the context. The avocational _lernen_ Heilman describes is such that the context defines the text, what people bring to the text dictates what the text will be permitted to say. That is why Heilman finds so much free association, so little attention to the issue at hand. The issue at hand is the Torah, and the task is to study the Torah. That by definition constitutes the program of the class room, the curriculum, the teacher's plan. If _lernen_ happens when "people come to class to get their feelings about Judaism off their chests," as Heilman says, the _lernen_ has nothing to do with Torah. It is something we make up as we go along.

To summarize this part of the argument: _lernen_ as Heilman portrays it and Talmud Torah as the classic texts of Judaism portray it bear slight resemblance to one another. That negative argument sets the stage for the positive proposition I wish to lay forth. It is, as I said, that those same attitudes that define our work in the secular academy also dictate how we should do our work in the sacred circle of Talmud Torah.

What we seek in our classrooms is for students not only to learn, but to learn _how_. It is not enough to master the facts. We want our students to know how people think, the methods, not only the results, of learning.

We seek, second, not merely to repeat knowledge but to renew learning. What this means is to rediscover the logic, the principles of order and structure, that dictate knowledge. For that purpose merely repeating what we know is never enough. Every good course promises to look for the new, leads students into the unknown. History 2 does not go over the immutable truths of History 1.

Finally, in our classrooms we come with a purpose in mind, and we do our best to carry out that purpose. The teacher's work requires more than the mere validation of the students' value. There is a prior, an overriding program of learning. The conception that, when we come together, it is to tell one another how we feel contradicts everything for which we stand. For the mind does its work only when it follows logic and discovers order.

Now when you turn to the texts that we study when we study Torah, what traits of mind do we discern?

First, in the Talmuds we find stress on the flow of argument, on the use of the critical intellect, on the promise of disagreement and critical discussion. Indeed, the two Talmuds and most of the writings that flow from them deal more with the _how_ of learning than with the _what_. The facts change from tractate to tractate. The methods of critical reasoning remain always uniform, everywhere operative and applicable. So, as I said, Talmud Torah demands more than merely erudite repetition of what everyone knows.

Second, the substance of Talmud Torah spreads out over an enormous number of books, a vast area of learning. By definition, standing still, repeating some one thing, will not do. The new and the unknown lie always before; no one masters the whole. Everyone undertakes an unending voyage through the worlds of the Torah. The very character of the Torah dictates the purpose of Talmud Torah, and given the breadth and diversity of the Torah, no one can find satisfaction in repeating a few simple sayings.

And I hardly need to restate the simple fact that free-association and Talmud Torah are enemies of one another.

Since I find it self-evident that the character of the Torah and the traits of lernen bear nothing in common, I must ask why so vast a world today assumes that the true, the "authentic" mode of Judaic studies, of study of Torah, of lernen, emerges from the circles, in synagogues and in yeshivas, described by Heilman. How can people who claim to be the only ones who know "the Torah" and who insist they are the only ones with sufficient erudition to say what "the Torah" says also exhibit so little interest in the substance and the form of Talmud Torah as these emerge from the books of the Torah themselves? My best guess is that the emperor is simply naked. The great traditions of learning embodied in classical yeshivas, and embodied even in our own day in some yeshivas, have lost their hold on the bulk of Orthodoxy, as well as on those Conservative and Reform rabbis who use the same language and claim to teach the same texts in the same way. Heilman describes not so much yeshivas as circles of students formed by lay people in association with rabbis who once studied in yeshivas. He will find in Conservative and Reform synagogues analogous groups.

So far as Talmud Torah has been turned by the rabbinate into ritual learning, the fault lies not with the great yeshivas but with their inferior products. So far as rivers of unfelt words drown in free association all sense, order, and meaning in the sacred texts, the reason is that those who spew out the stream of words do not know how to speak sensibly and pointedly. In yeshivas and equivalent seminaries they did not learn. But that does not necessarily mean they were not taught. So far as people hold on to the known, which they repeat and cherish, it is because they know only a little, and have not got much to tell other people. So far as the teacher tolerates free association, it is because then his authority remains secure, despite his limited learning. The main thing is for everyone to feel good and be happy, feel holy and be reassured. For that purpose, learning scarcely matters; lernen is not about learning anyhow. So, in a word, lernen as Heilman describes it testifies to the inauthenticity of its practitioners. It tells us that they very thing they claim to know they do not really understand at all.

Yet, to conclude, may we in the academy, who study and teach Judaic texts, claim superiority over those who practice lernen in yeshivas, seminaries, synagogues, and temples?

So far as professors of Judaic Studies engage in ethnic celebration and see their task as repeating and reaffirming the kerygma of whatever Judaism they espouse, they too carry out ritual-learning.

So far as professors of Judaic Studies lay claim to special standing and engage in special pleading, treat the Jews as essentially different from other groups and analyze the Jews and Judaism through canons of inquiry and reason inapplicable elsewhere, they too practice lernen, not learning.

To the measure that the academic sector of Jewish learning defines its work as the reading of prescribed texts, with slight interest in the how but obsession only with the what, the academic sector is not better than the religious one. Indeed, it is worse, since the practitioners of lernen at least do not claim to do something different from what has traditionally been done, while the professors of Judaic Studies celebrate the difference.

Above all, to that degree that academic studies of the Jews and Judaism prove repetitive and unproductive, creative only of boredom, incapable of asking new questions and answering them in fresh ways, to that degree the allegedly secular goes over the ground of the supposedly religious and traditional teacher. In my view the state of Judaic Studies in the academy scarcely improves upon the level of lernen in yeshivas and synagogues, except in its remarkable pretense at secularity, sustained in a setting of nearly unrelieved ritualism.